Jo Hemmings was the UK's first Dating Coach and is a Relationship Coach and trained Behavioural Psychologist. She has a weekly celebrity body language column in *More* magazine and writes regularly for the national press. Jo makes regular appearances on BBC and Sky News as a celebrity psychologist and is also the co-founder of The Relationship Coaching Academy – the organisation that coaches the coaches. Her websites include: www.datingcoaches.co.uk, www.celebritypsychologist.co.uk and www.relationshipcoachingacademy.co.uk

How to Have Great Sex

Jo Hemmings

Vermilion
LONDON

1 3 5 7 9 10 8 6 4 2

Published in 2010 by Vermilion, an imprint of Ebury Publishing

Ebury Publishing is a Random House Group company

The Random House Group Limited Reg. No. 954009

Addresses for companies within the Random House Group can be
found at www.rbooks.co.uk

A CIP catalogue record for this book is available from
the British Library

The Random House Group Limited supports The Forest Stewardship
Council (FSC), the leading international forest certification organisation.
All our titles that are printed on Greenpeace approved FSC certified
paper carry the FSC logo. Our paper procurement policy can be found at
www.rbooks.co.uk/environment

Printed and bound in Great Britain by
CPI Mackays, Chatham, ME5 8TD

ISBN 9780091929282

Copies are available at special rates for bulk orders. Contact the sales
development team on 020 7840 8487 for more information.

To buy books by your favourite authors and register for offers, visit
www.rbooks.co.uk

Contents

Acknowledgements

This book has been huge fun to write and as I was extremely anti-social while putting it together there are lots of people that I'd like to thank for bearing with me as well as those who have been of invaluable help in providing revealing stories of their own sex lives as well as toys and games to test out.

Forgive me for those I have missed out but really special thanks must go to my best gal pals who have kept me going by dragging me away to drink white wine, under feeble protest, and those who had faith in me that there was life after manuscript deadline.

Very special thanks go to my lovely neighbour and close friend Chris who ensured that I finished my weekend's work by relaxing and watching the very gentle and not-so-sexy *Lark Rise to Candleford* on a Sunday night. And to my wonderful and ever supportive girlfriends who make my holidays in lovely Fethiye so special as well as being the best company throughout the long winter months – Tina, Joanna, Clare, Carole, Katie and Emma. And Sarah and Rachel, Monica and Rob for being the best friends a girl could want.

I'd also like to thank my wonderful sons Matt and Ollie, mainly for being diplomatic and for the fact that while they were on my Mac, they were embarrassed enough to ignore draft chapters printed out and strewn over my desk. It can't have been easy for them . . .

I am very lucky to have some fantastic professional help and my heartfelt thanks and appreciation go to my enthusiastic and energetic agents, Amanda and Liz, and to my wonderful editor at Vermilion, Julia Kellaway, who managed to remain undaunted by an author who is also a Publisher!

The lovely Monique Carty at sextoys.co.uk has been very generous in supplying me with copious amounts of fun items to test out and I'd also like to thank Nikki at Nookii (how good do names get?!), Sara at Lelo, Suki at OhMiBod and the PR people at Philips, SaSi, Jimmyjane, Fun Factory, LoveHoney and Je Joue for all their help and advice. I recommend all these websites and list them at the back of this book – where would we be without the fun and pleasure that they provide?

Last, but most certainly not least, I would like to give much love and appreciation to my lovely man. In spite of problematic times, you have never baulked at a new toy or a new suggestion for play. You are my friend, my inspiration, my joy and my sublime pleasure. Thank you.

Introduction

'How to Have Great Sex.' It's a simple enough, if rather challenging promise. And you'll know when – or indeed if – you have enjoyed great sex, right? Well, no, in my experience, that's not exactly true. You can drive a fabulous car without knowing the workings of an engine and you can live in an amazing house without knowing how it was constructed. And you can definitely have pretty good sex without knowing much about the whereabouts of your G-spot or expanding your sexual repertoire beyond missionary and doggy style. But *great* sex? That needs a lot more detail on how everything works, how you and your partner are put together sexually and how to maximise your pleasure by putting it into practice.

What if you don't have sex or indeed have never had sex? Being a virgin, whether by choice or lack of opportunity, is actually much more common than the media would have us believe. Of course it will feel strange the first time that you have sex and it may or may not be great – sadly, as we get so wound up about our virginity, it tends to be the latter. However if this is you and you've bought this book (so I am assuming that you want to know about how to make it good for you, rather than a rushed, behind-the-bike-shed fumble) you've made a pretty good start in learning about your body, your responses and your pleasure zones. Make sure you choose a gentle, considerate and understanding partner and the chances are that they'll be just the same in bed.

A scanty level of sexually intimate knowledge along with predictability and a lack of attention to detail are the key elements of so-so sex. There's lots of sex talk about. We're happy to say that someone's good – or bad – in bed. We can chat about how fabulous oral sex is with Charlotte or Simon. But we generally don't go into blow-job-by-blow-job detail. It's just too explicit, and anyway where do you find the words to describe the pleasure without sounding too technical or smutty? Well, somewhere between the technical and the smutty lies a whole wealth of pleasure, fun, excitement and sexual skill that is yours for the taking and I hope you'll find just what you want in this book.

How to Have Great Sex is not a sex manual. It's not meant to be read from cover to cover. It doesn't generalise, skim over the 'embarrassing' bits or assume that you're a virgin or a superstud that needs a few extra ideas. It won't make you feel inadequate, underqualified or make your brain ache with technical jargon. It is simply a bunch of tried and tested ideas, tips and techniques to enhance your sexual pleasure, whether you are an experienced lover or just about to take the plunge. Great sex is about sharing fun, pleasure and gratification. And if I can offer just one or two alternatives that get you thinking they might just be worth trying, then that's my job well done.

As a behavioural psychologist and a dating and relationship coach who counsels couples on a regular basis, I know just how many people *expect* great sex to be borne naturally out of a great relationship. I also know that there isn't a great relationship that doesn't include great sex and that variety, regularity and a couple of essentials like oral sex and quickies can fade as rapidly as a spent erection once you become complacent in a relationship, however romantically loved up you are. Love can so easily replace lust and without lust where's the hot sex? And it's easy to fall into complacency and predictability when sex is on tap. The curses of a regular sex life – it can easily get repetitive, when we should be expecting much more in terms of quality as well as quantity. Above all, I believe, from having counselled many thousands of people, that great sex is not simply a bonus of a good relationship, it is fundamentally *essential* to maintaining a healthy relationship. And I also believe that great sex is not available to just a lucky few, it's there for the taking (with a little inside knowledge) for *every* one of us.

Perhaps the most important advice that you can take from what follows in this book, is that like anything else you practise on a regular basis, sex simply gets better the more that you do it!

So, above all, I want you to enjoy this book – find something different, new, challenging, exciting, wild and fulfilling – whether you're a novice just starting out on your sexual journey or a long-term couple looking for a few ideas . . .

Safe Sex

If this were a contract, then what follows would be the small print. The boring bit that you can't really be bothered to read because it just gets in the way of getting started. But you should take a moment out to read it, because it's the stuff that protects you from making unnecessary mistakes.

While this is a book about fun, pleasure and indulging and fulfilling your strongest needs and desires, sexual intimacy brings with it certain concerns – in both a physical and a psychological sense.

So, much as I am someone who has relatively few problems with the 'consenting adults, in the privacy of their own home' school of thought – and in fact positively encourage variety, imagination and a lack of inhibition – there are a few basics that need to be spelled out from the start.

Some of these warnings you will know or be aware of. Others may come as a surprise – especially if you're trying something new for the first time. And none are designed to inhibit the pleasure principle, even though they might seem to lack the spontaneity factor. Your most important sexual organ is your brain and how you use it. And it stands to reason that the more relaxed you are, by knowing that you and your partner are doing all you can to prevent sexually transmitted infections, pregnancy and unwanted pain, the more likely you are to have great sex.

It's an unfortunate fact of life, that in spite of huge sums of money being poured into sexual information and advice, the statistics for HIV, viral and bacterial sexually transmitted infections – including chlamydia, herpes, pubic lice and gonorrhoea – are all going up. All this increases your chances of catching something pretty unpleasant.

Sadly, you can't judge someone's likelihood of carrying an STI from the way they look or the way that they dress, speak, the job they do or even what they might say. Indeed, many people are carriers of highly infectious and fertility-threatening – or even life-threatening – diseases without even being aware of it.

Always remember, that however personally responsible you are and however good your intentions to make sure that you are protected during sex, drinking too much can lead to a greater risk of carelessness. Alcohol – and certain other recreational drugs – seriously lower your resistance to think responsibly, so while a drink or two is a great social lubricant, just be aware of your own limitations.

Condoms

Gone are the days, mercifully, when buying, carrying and using condoms held any kind of embarrassment. And if you do still feel embarrassed by doing any of these things, you need to wise up fast and take some responsibility for your own – and your partner's – sexual health.

Unless you are in a relatively long-term relationship – and in my view it's probably at least three months until you can feel safe enough to go without – you should always use a condom during penetrative vaginal sex. Longer, of course, if you're not using any other form of reliable birth control. Even if you're not having full penetrative sex, you should still use a condom, as there are enough germs at the tip of an erect penis to cause infection without penetration or ejaculation.

If you are having penetrative anal sex, a condom is even more important as, unlike the self-cleansing vagina, your bottom is a human waste-disposal unit and is a powerhouse of germs. You should use a non-spermicidally lubricated condom with extra water-based or silicone lubricant at all times. The anus is a much drier area than the vagina, and without sufficient lubrication there's a real danger that a condom could tear or burst.

Contraception

It may be the case that you want to enjoy great sex with your partner in order to fall pregnant, in which case this is entirely irrelevant to you. But if you don't – or aren't sure – then it is obviously essential to get you or your partner protected from conceiving while having sex. Apart from the obvious, effective contraception – whatever your personal choice of technique – will enable you to relax and enjoy sex that much more, without the added worry or complications of avoiding penetrative ejaculation. Terminating an unwanted pregnancy is not a recommended form of contraception and the morning after pill, useful as it might be in emergencies such as a split condom, is absolutely not the answer to careless sexual practice.

So my simple advice is to visit your GP for more information, buy a plentiful supply of condoms and lubrication and appreciate that great sex is even greater once you have dealt with the contraceptive responsibility that goes with it.

Foreplay

Generally thought of being a 'safe' form of sex, fingers can carry all sorts of germs, especially if the skin has been cut or has any form of lesion. If in any doubt, use waterproof plasters, especially if the foreplay involves anal touching or is during a woman's period. You can even bring a bit of 'doctor or nurse and patient' fun to this by using a condom over one or two fingers or latex gloves. It's also important to wash your hands after anal foreplay.

Oral sex brings its own potential set of problems, infections and germs. You can buy dental dams for extra protection. A dental dam is an ultra-thin latex sheet that you can put over your genitals or anus and helps create a barrier to infection. Like condoms, they can actually enhance, rather than detract from, sex and come in a variety of flavours.

Masturbation

Now this should be the safest form of sex, right? Well, in essence it is of course, but poor hygiene – such as unwashed hands – can actually spread genital infections such as gonorrhoea or chlamydia to the eyes for example.

Sex toys

These need to be thoroughly washed after each use – especially if you're using them on multiple partners. If they're water-proof you can simply use a flannel and some hand wash. If not, use cleansing wipes – baby wipes are ideal. If you're using anything that might draw blood, such as whips or chains, then these need extra attention in ensuring that they remain as pristine as possible.

Safe words

Even with the best will, longing and imagination in the world, some sexual practices will cause you more pain than you bargained for. And others you may simply not like. It's all a matter of experimentation between you and your partner. But given that you are not always going to be able to indicate your dislike or pain to your partner, mid-moan, you should agree to work out a 'stop now' word. 'Please stop' or even 'no more' aren't great words as these can be part of some of your role play and fantasies, so agree on a non-feeling descriptive word such as 'notebook' or 'radio'! And don't allow yourself to feel prudish about stopping some-thing that is no longer pleasurable.

Some of the techniques, ideas and suggestions in this book don't always seem to lend themselves to safe-sex practices. But while I promise not to go on about them – I've said my bit now – it is critical that you take responsibility for your own sexual health and that of your partner. While many of the delights that I hope you are going to uncover in this book would definitely not be deemed 'sensible' by some pleasure-principle kill-joys, practising safe sex – especially during the first few months of a relationship – should be simple common sense.

Let the fun begin . . .

1 Sexual Chemistry, Sex Appeal and Seduction

Sexual Chemistry

Before you can have truly great sex – and sustain the enjoyment of great sex – you have to have sexual chemistry. But what is this mysterious thing called sexual chemistry? You can't mix it up in a lab and you definitely can't buy it over the Internet – whatever your spam box tells you.

In its simplest form, sexual chemistry is that 'I'm not sure why I fancy him but I do' factor. It's the world's way of ensuring that we don't all fancy the same type or even the same person.

If you just want sex, because you're feeling a physiological longing or are involved professionally in the industry and it's what you do for a living, it's perfectly possible to have sex without sexual chemistry. It's also possible to have decent sex as a marital 'duty', because it's a Sunday morning and the kids are out and that's what you do or because you want to please your partner. But if you want passionate, intense, all-over tingling 'wow' factor sex – then sexual chemistry is critical. It's also what sees us through the difficult parts of a relationship.

Chemistry without lifestyle compatibility can pose problems in the long run. If common goals, social status and mutual interests aren't there, then sometimes the real world kicks in and the relationship can dwindle. However, deep chemistry is such a bond that a strong and enduring sexual passion often justifies making more compromises on other fronts, so be less demanding outside of the bedroom and just go with the flow in lifestyle terms. On the other hand, if you've met someone who you really like and ticks all your boxes in terms of desired career, lifestyle, background and so on but you just don't really fancy them, they are very likely to stay simply a friend. You could date them and accept that the chemistry isn't there for you, but you can't expect the sparks to fly if you didn't feel that primeval urge pretty early on. You can't make chemistry happen and sometimes it's incredibly annoying that this otherwise perfect partner just doesn't pop your toast, but that's chemistry for you. Unpredictable, uncontrollable and sometimes inappropriate.

Sexual chemistry can't guarantee you a lifetime of love, but it's a massive support structure when the relationship is experiencing a down time and hugely rewarding and fun when you're going through the good times. And if you don't have sexual chemistry with your partner but you're in a sensible, pleasant and otherwise rewarding relationship and neither of you mind sex being a chore, bore or not necessary at all, then stick with what suits you.

But for most people it's a critical element of finding a

mate. There's a multi-million-pound industry based on helping us find our mate via the Internet, singles events or professional matchmaking businesses. If all this was as simple as finding someone roughly our own age with a similar lifestyle who doesn't live too far away, then the industry might as well pack up and go home. The truth is that the industry survives because finding a partner with whom you find a potentially enduring sexual chemistry, just isn't that easy.

Mate selection is a highly complex process. And we are only consciously aware of a small part of it. Some of it is that low-lying level of consciousness, that draws us to someone but we're not always sure why. We often fancy people like this in 'clusters'. So if slightly vulnerable, unreconstructed men who look like Colin Firth or Kenneth Branagh do it for you, or dark-haired, luscious-lipped lovelies like Cheryl Cole or Angelina Jolie are your kind of woman, then you start to form a 'type' and there's already a heightened awareness when you meet someone who looks similar. I call that our Attraction Awareness Radar, as it lies part in the conscious mind and part in the sub-conscious.

Then, we have the fully conscious part of sexual attraction. This is rarely due to looks alone, but involves other critical characteristics such as sense of humour, voice or creativity. These are a unique chemical template that is special to each individual and helps create a longer lasting and sexual chemistry.

The rest of sexual chemistry operates at a sub-conscious level and is dictated by all sorts of uncontrollable factors such as hormones, pheromones and lust. More of which in due course . . .

Attraction Awareness Radar

Scientific research has shown us, time and time again, that there are certain things that we all find attractive. Men tend to fancy women with features that suggest youth and fertility, including a low waist to hip ratio, full lips and soft facial features. Women are attracted to classic signs of virility, taut bodies, broad shoulders and well-defined masculine facial features. Traditionally, women are also drawn to power, wealth – or the ability to achieve it – and intelligence. These basic factors are all signs of sexual potency and good gene stock.

This is all well and good if you're looking for sex as a reproductive process. But what happens when you want great sex just for the sake of it? For the pleasure principle. Then we see ourselves forming a different pattern of attraction awareness. We form a certain type of person that's pleasing on the eye to us and we look to see if there are other compatibility factors that help us make that giant and oh-so rare step into true sexual compatibility.

Understanding sex appeal

What makes someone sexy? Well, firstly it has pretty much nothing to do with how tight a guy's trousers are or how many buttons are undone on his shirt. And not that much to do with silicone F cups spilling over either. And secondly, it doesn't have all that much to do with their looks. It's a bit like chemistry – it's different things to different people and it isn't necessarily the dishiest, most stylish person in the room who is sexy to you. They will be someone who looks like they love people, love sex and could be seriously hot in bed.

YOU'RE ON YOUR WAY TO BEING SEXY IF . . .

- You're not fixated on your looks, ensuring that every hair is in place or that you have just shaved within an inch of your life. Being relaxed in your own body is very sexy.
- You're fun. You won't be the bar-room joke teller, but you'll have an infectious enthusiasm and zest for life and a smile that will make someone go weak at the knees.
- You're genuinely interested in other people. You'll listen to what people have to say with genuine enthusiasm and make them feel special.
- You're confident. You won't be afraid to speak your mind, even if your views are occasionally controversial.
- You understand and use eye contact in just the right amounts. You won't stare but will hold someone's eyes just enough to make them feel wanted and special.
- You're tactile in just the right amounts. A gentle stroke of the arm, perhaps, or a hug and a hello kiss that brushes your cheek, not just the air. You won't pinch someone's bum, or give him or her a sloppy, wet kiss.

What works for you?

So, what conscious factors combine to cause the riot of hedonism and pleasure for you? Perhaps you haven't yet identified them. But they're worth giving some serious thought to, because along with your Attraction Awareness Radar and the heady brew of hormones and pheromones, they form the recipe that's going to put you in the best possible place to enjoy the most fulfilling sex of your life.

Very broadly, sexual chemistry is a combination of looks, voice and humour. It can happen in an instant or it can take a little while to develop. It can start off by simply fancying someone and grow into an extraordinary desire that we are barely able to control. It isn't love – it is much more primeval than that. It may be a mixture of things about them – someone's eyes, the way they smile or tenderly brush your cheek when you're feeling low. It may be the way they dance, their gentle but strong voice or their ability to make you laugh. But it won't be their bank balance, flashy job or mutual love of modern art, it's far less definable and material, that's for sure. You can't have chemistry with someone that you've never met either. You might drool over photos of the latest celeb heartthrob, but you can't feel chemistry for them, because you have never met them and never encountered the whole person. Chemistry sometimes attracts us to seriously unsuitable partners and is pretty hard to resist once it kicks in. It gives you butterflies in the pit of your stomach, makes your head spin and can give you the highest of highs. It's lust at first sight and when it happens it can take your breath away. It's dangerous, wonderful, and powerful and frankly, it's scary, because it's hard to control your feelings, even if you are just about able to control what you actually do about them.

It can happen when you meet your best mate's new partner, a married colleague or your new boss. In these sorts of instances you'll need all your inner strength to make your head rule your heart. But if it happens when you meet someone who is unattached, available and who is clearly attracted to you too, then harness all that delicious passion and lust and just enjoy!

Unlike lust, chemistry rarely wanes and if you discover that just having a coffee with someone or catching them reading a newspaper makes you feel waves of desire, you probably have the makings of a good and enduring relationship on your hands. Chemistry in the bedroom can make sex sizzle big time. It makes you feel sexy, excited, passionate and uninhibited. It also makes you a great pleasure giver. You want to make this person as happy and as satisfied as they make you feel.

So we have defined this mysterious chemical reaction as a sort of emotional DNA. A highly charged and powerful reaction to someone that might defy our expectations and hopes or might, with luck, kick in at just the right time with the right person.

Hormones – and Other Sub-conscious Stuff

There is a mass of research out there on how our hormones affect our sexual chemistry. Some of it is truly fascinating – much of it is seriously tedious (especially as there is little if anything that we can do to control what happens as a result of hormonal attraction) particularly when we just want to get someone's kit off and get stuck in!

But as it's such a critical part of what makes us sexually attracted to someone else and has a starring role in how much we enjoy sex, it would be a dereliction of duty for me not to mention just a few of these studies. So, here are my top three amazing sexual hormone facts to entertain you in those moments when getting down to it just isn't possible or practical.

- *MHC (Major Histocompatibility Complex)*
  A very unsexy name that basically means that we choose suitable sexual mates by smell. We literally sniff out partners who have dissimilar MHC genes in order to produce healthier babies with better-developed immune systems. Interestingly, taking the pill confuses this scent for women and they tend to go into reverse – choosing a mate whose MHC genes are more similar to them which means they're less likely to produce such healthy offspring. And you thought that it was their eau de toilette that attracted you in the first instance . . .

- *Ovulation bias*
  Studies have shown that men tend to find women more attractive as they near ovulation, while women during their ovulation period prefer more masculine men. At other stages in their cycle, when ovulation hormones are not dominant,

women are more attracted to other less physical qualities in a man, such as intelligence or ability. This is due to the release of more oestrogen at this point in the cycle. Interestingly, scientists also found that by applying a little make-up during the low oestrogen periods, men become easily confused and there is no difference in their attraction levels!

- *Oxytocin*

  This is a hormone released after sex, which gives you that warm, fuzzy, can-life-be-any-more-perfect feeling. It is the hormone that kicks in during childbirth and helps a mother bond with her newborn. It creates a false feeling of love that has led many a couple to confuse this feeling of contentment with true love.

Who put the moan in pheromones?

Pheromones are an even more complex type of hormone than those above and while they are used in assisting many animals to find the perfect mate (it's why cats go crazy when they smell catnip, for example) they are also one of the most sexual hormones in humans too.

They are released in very small quantities through the sweat glands in the armpits and groin, but it's the pheromones produced from the glands in the vagina and on the head of the penis that are the most potent in sexual attraction. Interestingly, while these almost indefinable scents that these pheromones produce may be attractive to one person, they smell quite repellent to another!

A substance called androstenol (no one said that the science of sex was sexy!) has been established as the key sexual pheromone. Similar to testosterone (now that one, you have heard of!) it is secreted by both men and women and is the stuff that is put into perfumes, after-shaves and soaps to help us attract the perfect partner. Given that these smells are highly individual and personal and one size does not fit all, you can see why these don't really fulfil their lavish promises.

Perhaps the most interesting thing about androstenol is that it's responsible for 'menstrual synchrony' – the reason why women's periods begin to coincide, timing wise, when they are living in closed communities or simply working closely together.

So, you can see that behind the scenes, sexual hormones that we are not even aware of play their part in attracting a mate as well as linking people together sexually, through fertility, in close communities, thereby ensuring the greater continuance of that community.

Sexual Performance

Let's go onto what bothers us much more than hormone secretion or the subconscious factors of sexual chemistry: the concerns that we all have over sexual performance. The bitter irony about sexual performance is that the more we worry about it, the less likely sex is to make us feel satisfied. I don't even like the word 'performance'. It implies some sort of staged entertainment where your audience will judge you on any particular night. To a degree sex is a show, I guess, although the most interactive show where pleasure rather than performance matters most. Having stage fright will make you clam up (literally in some cases, when the vagina goes into a tight spasm called vaginismus) and the best performers are the most relaxed ones.

Sexual performance will fluctuate during any relationship. Sometimes you will be totally up for it and behave like a wild cat in bed and at other times you'll want a more sensual sort of lovemaking. Tiredness, stress and hormones all affect our performance in bed. Men may find it difficult to raise or sustain an erection and women may not always have an orgasm.

This book is designed to give you reassurance and inspiration. It should be a trusted bedside friend who won't let you down and will always give you something new to try and show you another way you might not have thought of. But we all vary in sexual performance from time to time. While one swallow does not make a summer – metaphorically and orally – there will be times when the section on masturbation pleases you most or foreplay becomes endplay. The varieties of how this book works for you should be endless. Keep your sex life fresh with fantasies, a little kinky stuff if it suits you and never be afraid to say when something doesn't feel right or hurts.

Size issues

Most of us have been brought up believing that the size difference between one person's genitals and another's isn't that great and any size difference doesn't really matter. That men's penises are pretty much all the same when erect, even if they look different in their flaccid state, and that as a woman's vagina is flexible enough to expand to get a full-term baby's head through, so they can accommodate any size penis. Most of this is myth, I am afraid.

Genitals, in both sexes, vary considerably. Men often fret that their penis is too small and women fret that their vaginal canal is too big. For those men that like to be reassured, the average length of a flaccid penis is 8.6–9.3 cm and the average length of a fully erect penis is between 12.9 and 14.5 cm. The average girth, or circumference, of a fully erect penis is between 8.8 and 10 cm. So now you know. And if you're really worried you could go to the drastic and hugely expensive options of having plastic surgery to enhance your penis size or tighten your vagina.

But the truth is that we fall in love with a whole person, not just their vagina or penis. And sex, as I hope you'll have gathered by now, is so much more than simple penetrative intercourse. Maybe it's true that a guy with a (supposedly) smaller penis tries harder and is more accomplished at oral sex. Maybe the same could be said for women with a bigger vagina. Maybe not. The truth is that there is a variance in size and sometimes this causes discomfort or concern, so let's look at the ways of working around it, as discovering size incompatibility with someone you're otherwise delighted to be with, should never be a deal breaker.

Your vagina is too small

This is a common concern for women who have never experienced vaginal childbirth. And there is a condition called vaginismus, where the vagina goes into spasm and prevents penetrative sex at all. This is usually due to psychological issues, often stemming from a fear of sex or an unfortunate parental attitude towards sex or even abuse as a child, and there is help out there if you need it. When we were virgins we were all pretty tight, but what if you're just built that way? A long penis can hurt during penetration because it can hit the cervix. A wide penis may feel like it's stretching you too much and it can also lead to bacterial infections if it's rubbing against your urethra.

The main cause of discomfort is lack of **arousal**. You need to have plenty of foreplay to get aroused and to allow your vagina to self-lubricate, get engorged and expand. And it's not just physical stimulation that you need – you need to be mentally and emotionally aroused too. At the tail end of a relationship, or during a bad patch, women often report that intercourse becomes more uncomfortable due to the fact that they don't feel as emotionally aroused as they once did. Adding more clitoral stimulation or using a vibrator can be a fun and effective way to ensure that you are in the right mood physically as well as emotionally.

Use a good dollop of **lubricant** too. Even if you haven't needed to use lubricant with previous partners, it is the single most effective thing you can use to ease discomfort due to a penis that feels too large for your vagina. And during menopause or times of ill-health or anxiety, the vagina tends to become less self-lubricating. These days there are loads of different brands of lube available and they all make sex more comfortable and fun by making it more slippery. Experiment with a few different kinds to see if a thicker or thinner lube is best for you and your partner.

There are also different **positions** that you can adopt which will maximise the size of your vagina during sex. Spreading your legs wide and bending your knees a little, while pressing your bottom down on the bed, will help relax the vaginal muscles and make penetrative sex easier. Encourage your partner to tease you a little and enter a little bit at a time, rather than a full and instant thrust, which can be a bit of a shock to the smaller vagina! If he stages his entry, this will make you feel a lot more comfortable as well as encouraging you to create your own lubrication.

Try to avoid positions that give deep penetration, like doggy-style sex, and go for positions where you can assume more control, like sitting astride your lover. As with anything else, enjoy experimenting and keep the lines of communication open so that your partner knows what feels good and what gives you the undesirable 'ouch' factor.

Your vagina is too big

Some women are just built with fairly loose vaginal muscles, whereas others had no problem until they had children, and the problem seemed to become progressively worse with each subsequent baby. This causes a lack of sensation and pleasure during intercourse because the tension needed to hold the penis in place and 'massage' the walls of the vagina simply isn't there.

The good news is that there are exercises that you can do to rectify the problem, although you will need to do them on a regular basis.

Pelvic floor exercises – or Kegel exercises as they are sometimes known – are, once you've mastered the basics, an easy to do vaginal muscle workout that can make a huge difference and can be done discreetly any time and anywhere. They are cheap (free, in fact!); effective and can be done when sitting, standing or lying down. Pelvic floor exercises strengthen the muscles around the pelvis and make for a tighter vagina as well as giving you the show-off factor that he'll love, as you squeeze them around his penis during sex.

The muscles are easy to identify. Try taking a pee and in mid flow, try and stop the flow of urine. Do this a couple of times and you'll quickly begin to recognise the contractions needed – these are your pelvic floor muscles. If you're having any trouble feeling them, insert a finger into your vagina and squeeze around that. You should be feeling an upward and inward contraction, rather than a feeling of bearing down.

When you're doing the exercises, make sure that you don't hold your breath or tighten the muscles in your tummy, thighs or bottom or you'll be exercising the wrong muscle groups!

You need to be doing around 40 of these exercises a day. Not as scary as it sounds as you can do them while sitting at your desk or driving a car. You should do around 20 slow contractions and around 20 faster contractions.

During the slow contractions you should lift your pelvic floor muscles to a count of ten and hold them tight for a count of ten too. You might find that you can't hold the contractions for so long at first so build up to it over a few weeks. You should get to a stage where you can do 10 at a time of these slower contractions and ultimately 20 at a time after a few weeks.

Fast contractions also give your pelvic floors a tight workout, but can be more difficult so don't push yourself too hard at first. It takes around three months of doing these exercises daily to see any noticeable effect – this is not an overnight solution. Fast contractions consist of lifting your pelvic floor muscles quickly, holding them for one second and then releasing them for one second.

There are also **positions** that you can adopt to give you maximum sensitivity and not surprisingly, these are pretty much the opposite of the positions that you should try if you have too small a vagina. Doggy-style or rear-entry sex is a good one to try, as is any position where your partner is entering at an angle or slant. Squeezing your thighs together during sex can also help contract the vagina wall and give you greater feeling and sensitivity.

Your penis is too small

Even if you're convinced that your penis is way too small, compares unfavourably to your locker room pals and is the bane of your life, it probably isn't. If you fear that you'll get laughed at by your next partner or she'll utter those dreaded words 'are you in there yet?' it probably won't happen. But you've grown up thinking that the size of your manhood determines your manlihood and that's a difficult belief to eradicate overnight. So let's deal with the here and now. If you are – or perceive yourself to be – a bit on the small side, what can you do about having great sex?

If you've flicked to this page straight away, you may not have noticed a theme repeated many times in this book, so let me make something crystal clear. Most women do not achieve orgasm through **penetrative sex** alone. In fact, most women don't even need to *have* penetrative sex to reach orgasm. And most women (yes, I know it's getting repetitive) say that they prefer oral sex to penetrative sex. So unless your tongue also has a size issue, you should be able to satisfy your lover as well as any 'better' enhanced guy. And it's not just oral sex that pleases a woman – it's massage, genital masturbation and all sorts of other tricks that you can perform with your mouth, tongue and hands. Penetrative sex is simply part of lovemaking and not necessarily the bit that is likely to make your woman come to a climax and sigh with pleasure.

You might find that you come too quickly. This is a combination of the psychological – your nerves and performance anxiety get the better of you – and the physiological. If you do have a smaller than average penis, then the chances are (unfair, I know . . .) that your nerve endings are concentrated over a smaller area, the head of your penis, and this can make you climax too quickly. The answer is to **masturbate** more frequently. This encourages you to desensitise the head of your penis and is especially useful to do within an hour prior to sexual intercourse, as you'll tend to last longer the second time around.

Adopting the right **positions** to maximise your size and sensitivity will also help. Any positions where you can thrust more deeply will help; so doggy style is a good one as the slant of her vagina means that it's likely to be a tighter fit. Any angled position, rather than the direct entry of the missionary position for example, will help make her vagina feel tighter as will her legs inside your legs during the missionary position, as this encourages her vagina to close up a little.

Your penis is too big

Yes, I know this is the stuff of porno films and the belief is that every man would like to be hung like the proverbial donkey, but some men really do suffer from an excessively long penis, or an over-wide penis, or a mixture of both. And for some women this can be seriously uncomfortable, in spite of the vagina being able to expand to deliver a baby.

Make sure that your partner is fully **aroused** before having penetrative sex. That means paying special attention to genital masturbation and oral sex as well as helping her to relax emotionally, by making sure that the ambience is right. You might find it more difficult than your less well-endowed friends to enjoy a quickie, due to a lack of arousal, but using a decent dollop of lubrication might help overcome this problem. This will not only help make her feel more slippery and less tight, it will also avoid the burning sensation that you might get due to her vagina being too tight for your size.

Also adopt **positions** that involve less deep penetration and less constant thrusting. Some of the *Kama Sutra*-type intimate positions, described later in this book, will help. Also having her sitting astride you, or lying side by side, will give her more control, meaning that she's less likely to feel nervous about you going too far in. Use gentle, part-penetrative movements before going deep inside her. If she has a short and narrow vaginal canal, and you have a long and wide penis, you may find that you never actually achieve full-length penetration, but this shouldn't affect either of your orgasms or ultimate pleasure.

Sex drives

We all go off sex from time to time and if you've been out of a relationship for a long time, you may have got very used to living without sex and not feel that it is essential to your well-being. Alternatively you could be as horny as hell and regularly wake up wet between the thighs having enjoyed a sleep-time orgasm.

But what if your sex drives really don't seem to match? She is on high sexual alert any time, anywhere, any place and he likes sex on a Sunday morning only. Or he might see sex as high on the agenda as food or water or sleep while she enjoys it, but hey, not all the time. Sometimes you just want a cuddle in bed, or to watch TV or read the paper. What can you do about mismatched libidos? It's important to do something, otherwise your relationship will be doomed. A mutually compatible sex life is critical to the success of almost every relationship.

It's important to recognise that it isn't the fault of the

person who has the lower sex drive, even though it's often perceived as their problem. Sex drive is influenced by all sorts of factors – genes, hormones, lifestyle, mood and past experiences. However, it is important to meet in the middle somewhere, so that both partners feel satisfied.

It may be that you have never had a particularly high sex drive, in which case it's important to make this clear from the start. While many people will find this a major problem, others will accept it and even welcome the fact that they are released from the pressure of having to behave like a stallion on a constant basis. If, however, your sex drive has taken a sudden or recent and unexpected downturn, it is worth addressing some of the reasons why.

SEX DRIVE KNOW-HOW

- Your sex drive can ebb and flow, like the tides, for a variety of reasons including stress, fatigue, medication, pregnancy, the menopause, previous sexual traumas and hormonal imbalances. Poor diet, working too hard and dramatic weight gain or loss can also affect your libido.
- We tend to feel hornier in the spring, on long, light warm sunny evenings, when we are happy at work and for us women, just before our periods.
- Maybe your partner is not the right sexual partner for you. You may get on brilliantly with them but is he or she doing it for you sexually? He or she might just be a poor lover or you might not have the all-important chemistry to help your sex life sizzle.

- Has your sex life become drab of late? Maybe you're not putting enough effort into sex. Maybe your partner isn't. It's time to communicate your needs and wants, either in the sack or just by having a chat. It's important that your partner is aware of your concerns. This is where working through this book – or just dipping in and out – will help bring the zing back to your sex life.

- Sometimes we come across someone that has totally different sexual views to us. You may prefer to make love under the covers, lights dimmed, and prefer sex in the evening to the morning. They might want to have sex outdoors or in the broom cupboard at work, want you to play out their wildest fantasies or push you for anal sex. These problems can often be worked out by talking – and finding a level that suits you both. Then just keep building up the excitement by trying something new on a regular basis. You may well get to like it . . .

- Learn to feel sexy again. Flirt, indulge your own fantasies and get to know your own body intimately. Sometimes we lose touch with our own sex appeal and that affects our interest in the bedroom. Buy a decent vibrator or other sex toy (see page 215) and get to know more about your orgasms. Above all it will help you both understand the difference between vaginal and clitoral orgasms and what feels good for you – so experiment.

- Understand what it is that you enjoy most in bed and make sure your partner knows that. Show them what kind of foreplay most excites you and the positions that make you feel fantastic. Make this part of sex play rather than a heavy talk.

- If you're in an inappropriate or difficult relationship guilt can hold back your sexual pleasure. If you're having an affair or you still have feelings for someone else, guilty feelings can restrain you in bed. You need to dump the already attached lover or learn to move your feelings on to enjoy all the sheer pleasure without the burden of emotional guilt. Take time to recognise and receive pleasure for pleasure's sake.

Good sex

Good sex has everything to do with relaxation, trust and communication and much less to do with the technical expertise or the stamina and staying power of an Olympic athlete. It's also to do with shared sexual appetites, libidos and compatibility outside the bedroom. Like a lot of things in life, practice can make perfect. Learn to experiment, indulge your fantasies, initiate sex and make sure that it's a high priority in your relationship from the outset. Remind yourself that pleasure is the ultimate goal and understand that the only thing keeping you from having the hot sex life you deserve is a lack of imagination and a willing partner . . .

Bad sex

What if your lover is just truly awful in bed? They might lack enthusiasm, be as predictable as the waxing and waning of the moon, just not seem that interested in sex or just want to get straight to the main event, always in missionary style and miss out on foreplay altogether. Time to talk. And make sure you talk outside of the bedroom. Telling them that they are a crap lover, while you are under the sheets, is always a bad idea, however frustrating it is. Tell them about the good things they do, or used to do. There must be some special things that please you – and if there aren't, then maybe it's time to re-evaluate this relationship altogether. Then pluck up the courage to tell them what you think you'd like to make sex even better. Read together – or alone at first – the sections of this book on foreplay, positions, orgasms and fantasy and role play. Don't throw a barrage of weird and wonderful suggestions at them – they'll probably baulk at that and get all resentful – but take it slowly, telling them that they could make your orgasms that much better if they'd spend a little time on oral sex, for example. Make sure that he or she is reminded of this the next time that you are in bed. Don't boss them about and bark instructions at them, but move their hand or head and make sure that he or she knows that your body is responding well. Make sex a priority and vary positions and places. Always missionary? Take control and sit on top of him. Always under the covers? Grab her for a quickie on the stairs. Neither of you are sure quite what to do about it? Reading this book together can be a revelation. Long gone is the coy, textbook-like sex manual. I tell you like it is, address the problems that *you* have with genuine understanding and practical help and show you a whole sexual repertoire that can make a big difference to your enjoyment.

Sex and Seduction – the First-time Basics

Sex is pretty easy to come by these days. If you want to go out on the pull to have sex that same night, there's hardly a bar or a club that won't offer up the opportunity if you persist hard enough. Saying that, I think not having sex straight away actually makes you a little bit more special. It says that you've given it a little thought before showing what a sexy lover you can be with the right person. It also implies that you want a relationship of some sort rather than a one-night stand, so if your pull was only after a quick shag, they can bail out of the pursuit without you feeling like shit the next day because they don't want to see you again.

Anticipation, teasing and flirting can all be really exciting before first-time sex. Making him or her wait a little will make them keener than ever if they're after a little more than a one-off romp under the duvet. We are also emotional creatures and however much we have trained ourselves to be equal, even one of the lads, we can't overturn nature. Women usually need to have a little more than just lust to make great lovers. Lust, chemistry and desire combined with a little knowledge about other compatibility factors will make us even sexier. And there may well be times when you have regretted having sex too soon, but I bet you can't think of many occasions when you wish that you had slept with someone earlier than you did!

OK, so here you are. The approach, the initial flirting and the date are coming to an end. And you are definitely going to sleep with him or her tonight. How are you going to ensure that it isn't a clumsy, awkward disappointing experience when you want it to be raw, exciting, exhilarating and have him begging for more? Let's deal with the preparation, the build-up and the sex itself.

The preparation

- Carry a packet of condoms with you. And use them. It's a joint responsibility to protect yourself from STIs (for more see page 4).
- Get the mood right. If it's back to your place, make sure that the bed is made and that your sheets are crisp and clean. Laundered sheets have an especially good feel when slipping under the duvet. Dim the lights or get a few scented candles burning. Play a little soft background music. Something sexy and slow – not too slushy or hip-hop!
- If your partner can't stay the night then make sure that you leave yourself plenty of time for sex. Don't leave it until half an hour before their cab is due or the last train is about to leave. They'll be clock watching and all their concentration should be on you.

The build-up

- Foreplay is really important. Unless you're having wham-bam-through-the-door-rip-their-clothes-off sex on the stairs (which of course, is absolutely fabulous the first time) then you should build up anticipation by using foreplay to its best advantage. And that means licking, sucking, kissing, touching and oral sex, all before you get to the penetrative stage. Get the excitement and anticipation going.

- Don't worry about being 'perfect'. This is not an exam and you're not being tested. This is about having fun and pleasure and there are bound to be a few, er, cock ups on the route to great sex!

- Don't feel pressured to show off your entire sexual repertoire on the first night. You might be able to adopt positions that an Olympic athlete would admire, or enjoy sex wearing a pink marabou blindfold and a whip, but there's no rush to show them everything all at once.

- Don't expect too much too soon. If he can't manage to get or sustain an erection or you get cramp midway through, that's the way it is sometimes. It takes a while to get to know someone else sexually and the first time is often not the best.

The sex

- Make your partner feel good. Whatever the quality of their performance, let them know what made you feel great. This will both turn them on and pave the way for a little more knowledge about what makes you feel excited in bed.

- Keep your sense of humour. Even if the sex is a disaster, laugh it off and tell them that practice makes perfect.

- Relax and enjoy. This is not the time to be worrying about cellulite or wobbly bits. You'll both be nervous and unsure of each other's bodies. If the mood is right and you ensure that you are giving him or her pleasure, they won't notice anything amiss, I promise.

- Don't ask them 'How was it for you?' or 'What do you reckon then?' Really good sex won't happen until a few sessions in. This is a time to explore, get to know each other and find out what excites you both.
- Don't fret if you don't come. To achieve an orgasm you have to be in perfect sexual harmony and it might well be too early for that. You also need to be able to totally relax and that isn't ever easy the first time.

OK, so we've established the basics of sexual chemistry, helped you understand what makes it happen and how it works for you, we're agreed that we're banishing bad sex into another place and we've dispelled a few sex myths that might restrain your fulfilment. Let the party begin . . .

2 Self-pleasure: Masturbate to Become a Better Lover

Going Solo

Masturbation – for both sexes, but especially for men – gets a lot of unwarranted bad press. In spite of being the most natural way of exploring your own body and discovering what feels good for you, it has been attributed to all sorts of distressing symptoms – from giving you spots, stunting your growth or making you go blind or insane. There are also various slang terms that are commonly used as insults – wanker, jerk and tosser just being a few.

In fact, masturbating is good for you. Not only does it help relieve stress, it also causes your body to release pleasure hormones, such as endorphins, which help you feel good and relaxed. A recent Australian study also showed that the more men ejaculate between the ages of 20 and 50, the less likely they are to develop prostate cancer. It seems that ejaculation prevents carcinogens building up in the fluid caused by the prostate gland. It also reduces the likelihood of phimosis (tightness of the foreskin) and can also help to correct a tight foreskin in the first instance.

But apart from the beneficial medical reasons for masturbating, the psychological reasons are even more compelling. By helping you to understand your own body and what turns you on, you are more likely to communicate better with your partner, enjoy sex more and avoid sex-related psychological problems. It's also far better to learn how to masturbate well, and create your own fulfilling orgasms, so that you might avoid some of the unpleasantness – both medically and psychologically – of having a one-night stand with a virtual stranger simply to relieve sexual tension.

Girls – the basics

Firstly, it's important to find a time and a place where you can have some uninterrupted peace. And that means taking the phone off the hook, turning off your mobile, drawing the curtains and making your space as private and as warm as possible. This is a time of total indulgence and interruptions and a chilly room can adversely affect the deliciousness of that orgasm you are working towards.

You need to acquaint yourself with your own body. While you may be used to looking at yourself in the mirror on a daily basis – and be quite comfortable with what you see, even while naked – your genitals are one part of yourself that are not immediately visible. Masturbating is much easier if you take all your clothes off as struggling to view your vagina in a mirror while constricted by tights or knickers can be a tricky and not very erotic experience! Angle the mirror so that you can see and feel your clitoris with your finger – it is situated at the top of your vagina and looks like a little broad bean and may feel hard or soft. It may also feel very sensitive to touch, which is just as it should be, because stimulating your clitoris will help towards your orgasm. You may feel a little dry, so use a good gel-based lubricant like KY Jelly to make yourself feel moister. Lubricants keep the whole genital area nice and slippery and are perfect for masturbating as well as adding sensation to your touch.

When you've found your clitoris, you may want to stimulate yourself in other ways before going onto the main event – it's just like self-foreplay. You can use body lotion or massage oil to stroke your breasts, neck, inner thighs – or anywhere on your body that makes you feel good, sexy and relaxed. Lie on your bed in a comfortable position and let your hands and fingertips, with their myriad nerve endings, do most of the work. You may want to keep your eyes open and watch yourself or you may want to shut your eyes or lie in a darkened room and allow your sense of touch to become even stronger. When you feel that your body has started to tingle and feel good, you may find that your breath becomes shorter or that stroking your nipples seems to have a direct effect on making your clitoris 'tick' just a little. This is all good as you're finding your erogenous zones and the connections between them. When you feel ready let your fingers drift towards your vagina and starting with your outer genitals rub, stroke and explore your labia with as little or as much pressure as feels good. You can apply a little extra lubricant or lick your fingers and use those to create a more moist and exciting feeling.

When you start to feel more stimulated and open, move your index finger onto your clitoris. It will probably still be covered by a small hood of skin, as it's just like a mini-penis with its own foreskin. It will feel sensitive, so keep up a steady rhythm with your finger and as you become more excited the hood will retract, leaving it feeling even more pleasurable and sensitive. Try moving your finger back and forth or in a circular motion, whatever suits you.

After a while, the sense of pleasure will begin to increase in intensity and you might want to increase the speed of your stroking or insert a finger or two inside yourself as you feel your excitement mounting. Try squeezing your vaginal muscles in and out to build the sensation. This heightened pleasure leads to the orgasm itself, which is like being washed over by waves of unmistakeable pleasure. It also sends the vagina into a series of spasms or contractions and may make your clitoris so ultra-sensitive that you can no longer touch it. This fabulous treat is one of the greatest pleasures in life – it's calorie-free, cash-free and should be totally guilt-free too.

Some women like to watch soft porn while masturbating or listen to some sexy music. Other like to masturbate by candle light or fantasise about a hot movie star or a past or present lover. It doesn't matter how outrageous or unlikely your fantasies are – that's what they are there for! And if moving around, moaning or thrusting against a pillow help bring you to climax, go right ahead and enjoy . . .

A warm, scented bubble bath is also another great place to masturbate. As is the sensuality of a power shower. And for those of you that have felt the thrill of a water jet from a Jacuzzi, taking you by surprise, you'll know how good that feels too. And there's something very exciting about learning to come while sitting in a public Jacuzzi! It's all a matter of trial and error to see where and what suits you best. And just like sex itself, don't get into an exact same routine, each time – keep trying new things. You'll find yourself stimulated and horny in a way you didn't think possible. And remember, what suits one woman might not be right for you. Anything goes when you're masturbating and provided that you follow basic hygiene and safety rules by not inserting anything dirty or sharp into yourself, your pleasures are guilt-free and all yours and yours alone.

Around 20% of women use a vibrator to help them masturbate. They come in all sizes (and shapes!) from a discreet, purse-sized 'bullet' or wand shape, to a giant penis complete with throbbing veins and helmet. In fact, some of them look terrifyingly scary and lifelike – just bigger, wider and made of a dodgy, squidgy flesh-coloured plastic! The Rampant Rabbit, made ultra famous by the *Sex and the City* girls, is one of the most popular vibrators as it provides both vaginal and clitoral stimulation, with it's little rabbit 'ears'.

There's no doubt that using a vibrator is an easy way to have an orgasm – it doesn't require much effort and just holding it firmly against your vagina may well bring you to a climax! While it doesn't teach you much about your own body or sexual skills and needs, it is a very convenient way of masturbating, especially if you're short of time. Many women find that they can climax within a couple of minutes while using a vibrator, so if a self-fulfilling 'quickie' is what you're after, they do the job perfectly. Interesting although they are generally designed to be inserted inside the vagina, like a real penis, the majority of women find that they are more stimulating when just using the tip against their clitoris. It can sometimes feel uncomfortable to try and put your own fingers inside yourself, so using a neat vibrator with varying speeds inserted inside yourself at the same time can feel fabulous. One of the best, which was one of the earliest vibrators available, goes under the slightly bizarre name of the Non-Doctor, but it's discreet, effective and a perfect size and shape for the job. Vibrators are good fun, easily bought over the Internet if you're feeling a bit embarrassed about buying one over the counter, and are brilliant to use when you're with your lover too. Men love the feeling of a vibrator on and around their genitals and many also like the feeling of a vibrator inserted in their bottom. Just make sure that you use plenty of lubrication and if he is going to do the same to you, make sure it is cleaned with a sterile wipe between sessions.

You can use a vibrator, for masturbation, by lying back and inserting it into yourself or lowering yourself down over it. You'll probably need to stimulate your clitoris first though – otherwise it will feel like having sex without any foreplay or stimulation and won't feel that comfortable. Use lubrication with it too. If you're experimenting for the first time with a vibrator, press it against your labia and hold it there, varying the pressure until you find a rhythm that feels good for you. You can lie down, stand up or kneel on the floor. The only limit is your comfort, excitement and imagination. There is much more on vibrators and other sex toys, including some personal recommendations, on pages 215–17.

Guys – the basics

Unlike women, most men don't even remember 'learning' to masturbate. Or when they first did it. It was a lifetime ago . . . and now it's part of day-to-day life. However, men tend to be more hung up on the reasons why they masturbate, rather than their finely honed techniques. Of course, you masturbate to relieve tension – sexual or otherwise – but I'll bet your first experiences made you feel guilty or dirty. And if not, then they were sure to be furtive. Sometimes men never lose that early guilt of fumbling under the bedcovers wishing that the relief would come as soon as possible. The trouble with this is not the sense of guilt itself, but getting used to coming in minutes – or even seconds – can lead to premature ejaculation when you're with a partner. It seems that you have brought yourself to orgasm so quickly over the years, that when you want to prolong the process during sex, you just can't perform as you would like.

Part of overcoming this problem is to alter the way that you masturbate. Doing it the same way that you did as a young teenager, can only lead to a swift and early orgasm. You need to learn to delay your orgasm. Not only will it bring you greater pleasure, but it will make a huge difference to both your lovemaking technique and your sexual self-esteem.

However, retraining yourself after many years of making yourself climax in the fastest possible time isn't always easy, but in this case it is possible to teach an old dog new tricks!

Like women, men enjoy fantasising when they masturbate. However, unlike women who tend to fantasise about one particular hot celeb, their current or recent partner or simply a familiar but daring role play, like a man in uniform taking them roughly from behind, men have a massive variety in their sexual fantasies. It depends on your day. You may have got an erection watching a girl on the train that morning and fantasise about her. Or the girl who sits next to you at work. Or your girlfriend blindfolded, tied up and being flagellated by another woman. Basically, you do whatever it takes to get there fast, furiously and satisfactorily.

So, what can I suggest to make your orgasms better, longer to reach and more satisfying? I wouldn't be so bold as to actually teach you how to masturbate. But I can make it better for you – especially if you want to prevent coming too quickly with a partner.

Most guys use the fist technique. They make a loose, open – or closed – fingered fist and with varying degrees of grip and speed they run that fist up and down the shaft of their penis. You tend to use the same hand, at least to start with, and with your palm facing the side of your penis, you start at the top and move down, in a pumping motion, towards the bottom of your penis. Your grip may become tighter as you move your hand over the tip of your penis, but in sensitive men, especially circumcised men, this is too much and your grip might loosen. You might start at the bottom of the shaft and work upwards. What really matters is the rhythm – maintaining this is the key to that sexual tension that brings you the most satisfying climax. Some men masturbate in front of a porn movie or magazine (although not as many as you might think!), in front of the mirror or lying on the sofa. But most guys prefer to lie on the bed with their legs flopped apart. You might enjoy holding or stroking your balls or rubbing the area between your testicles and your bum, known as the perineum. It's an area full of nerve endings and can be very sensitive.

You might use lubrication. While women like a gel-based lubricant, most men go for whatever is to hand – soap, shampoo, shower gel, hair conditioner or moisturiser. Don't use a household cleaner or anything else abrasive. (Yes, I know this sounds obvious but ask any casualty nurse or doctor and they will tell you all sorts of horror stories that happened while grabbing the first liquid that came to hand.) What is important is to use the rhythmical rubbing motion as a route to playing with your frenulum, the thin, flexible fold of skin on the underside of the head of the penis which joins the foreskin. Using a 'basket weave' action with your hands, fingers and palms, over your frenulum can increase pleasure and delay orgasm. Changing hands – and so breaking the rhythm – can also delay orgasm. As can avoiding thinking of the woman of your fantasies – try switching to thinking about something much more mundane. Grabbing your testicles as you're ejaculating or pinching the bottom of your shaft also makes the orgasm last longer.

Varying techniques when you're masturbating can help you understand the pleasures of your body, rather than just masturbation as an end to releasing sexual tension. Just like women, men enjoy masturbating in the shower or the bath as it is slippery, squidgy, sexy and very easy to clean up afterwards! It also makes it easy to find those other bits that might give you pleasure – your bum, anus, perineum and testicles. It's also easy to slip a finger up your anus, which can increase pleasure hugely.

And here's the good news – you can also delay premature ejaculation by masturbating more frequently. The more you wank, the less sensitive your penis becomes. If you can masturbate at least twice in a day before you plan to have sex that night, especially less than an hour or two before, I guarantee that you will take considerably longer to climax than might be usual.

However often you masturbate, you must remember that your penis is a delicate organ. Don't put anything into it – it will give you searing pain unless done professionally by a medically trained technician for clinical purposes!

10 BRILLIANT REASONS TO MASTURBATE

1. What else in life is calorie-, cash- and conscience-free, yet brings you so much pleasure?
2. It's a massive stress reliever, enabling you to be more relaxed and sleep better.

3. The more you do it, the more orgasms you're likely to have with and without your lover.

4. Knowing where your erogenous zones are and how best to play them, makes you a much more sensitive lover.

5. It helps you separate love from lust – and makes for healthier long-term relationships.

6. It's totally safe.

7. It's healthy – it improves your circulation, makes your skin glow, gives you bags of energy and improves your libido.

8. If you know how to pleasure yourself it makes you much less likely to hop into bed with an unsuitable lover.

9. It gives you the chance to experiment with what feels good without feeling silly or embarrassed.

10. It feels fabulous!

3 Fabulous Foreplay: Kissing, Touching, Oral Sex and Hand Jobs

Back in the bad old days, foreplay was considered to be something a man 'had' to do, in order to get his partner aroused enough to have sex with her. Thankfully, foreplay has now become an integral part of lovemaking – for both men and women. The message is pretty basic – if you want great sex, learn to give and get great foreplay. But somewhere along the way between a snog and full-on sex, some foreplay techniques have rather gone out of 'vogue'. Back in the day, when we took a lot longer to get from the first kiss to falling into bed with a partner, petting – as foreplay was then known – was what we had to be satisfied with for months, years even, before we could move on to full penetrative intercourse. While I am not suggesting that we go back to those days, it did make us more imaginative in terms of foreplay and it would be tragic to lose the skills that previous generations used to have a lot of fun. Somewhere between kissing and full sexual intercourse could be found the mysteries of petting (generally a bit of touching and breast fondling, usually over a girl's bra) and the even more mysterious and slightly scary sounding 'heavy' petting. While it sounded like a term better suited to a keen dog owner stroking a St Bernard, heavy petting involved getting under a bra or panties, touching and playing with the naughty bits and maybe getting seriously 'heavy' by actually indulging in a little oral sex. However we choose to refer to it, foreplay is literally playing before sexual intercourse – whether that lasts all of a few minutes or happens intermittently over a much longer period of time, before we first experience penetration.

So, all well and good, but exactly what is foreplay? Foreplay is anything and everything that builds up arousal enabling you to have better sex. Undoubtedly, the best foreplay stimulates our most important organ: the brain. Without mind teasing and an aroused response due to our brain telling us that we want more, foreplay can be clumsy, unfulfilling and uncomfortable – even painful. Simply telling your partner that they are gorgeous and sexy gives them the security and excitement essential to great foreplay, without involving any physical contact at all. Foreplay can encompass flirting, teasing, seduction, eye contact and stripping, watching porn movies and feeding your lover sensuous foods like strawberries dipped in molten dark chocolate. Foreplay may or may not enable you to reach an orgasm. You may use foreplay to bring your partner close to an orgasm or just for basic stimulation. Or use it to give him or her an orgasm without moving onto penetrative sex.

Foreplay isn't something you tack onto the beginning of

sex to prolong the experience or to prove that you're considerate. Or – and there are some very bad lovers out there – something you do because you're expected to create some sort of razzmatazz before the main event. It's a sensuous, passionate and physiologically necessary part of sex. It deepens intimacy and promotes emotional connection, both so important for satisfying sex. Without foreplay a woman is likely to have a drier vagina due to lack of stimulation, and this can cause discomfort and pain, as well as an ultimately unsatisfying emotional experience. For a man, foreplay helps prevent premature ejaculation and impotence as well as creating harder erections with longer staying power.

And it's a truth universally known (as Jane Austen might have said in more liberal times) that women generally want more foreplay than they get. I have never counselled a female client who ever complained that her partner spent too much time on foreplay. And in the interests of a balanced approach, the one act of foreplay that men want more than anything from a woman is oral sex – fellatio – which is why I have paid special attention to this, later in this chapter.

Foreplay isn't prescriptive. It should vary from partner to partner and from sex session to sex session. It is part instinct, part learned behaviour – the more you practise and the more variety you introduce into your foreplay, the more it will help you to trust your instincts and learn new things. Practiced couples don't use foreplay as *fore* play at all. They create a wonderful repertoire where they have oral sex, for example, during sex. They'll have penetrative sex and break up their lovemaking session with oral sex or masturbation in order to keep the session as hot and prolonged as possible. And not all sex needs to involve foreplay either. While a quickie on the stairs with your partner might not actually involve sexual foreplay as we traditionally understand it, the preceding build up of intimate looks, a little flirting over dinner or on your journey home or some dirty talk or texting will all have contributed to the arousal and desire that you feel when you can't wait to get through the front door and get down to it. Quickie sex is a seriously underrated part of any sexual repertoire (more on page 109) but I want to give some detail on the kind of sexual foreplay that generally stimulates and arouses as an overture to a longer bout of making love.

Foreplay isn't about pressing the right buttons in the right order – in fact it definitely isn't about doing everything just the way you did it the last time, however fabulous that may have been. It isn't about tweaking nipples as if you're tuning an old-style radio, or about pulling hard on your man's penis to get him to a rock-hard erection in the fastest possible time. It's about understanding what gets your partner hot and delivering the goods that give them ultimate pleasure. It's also about anticipation itself – just imagining what your partner is going to do to you when his hand or her tongue, or simply their eyes, start to drift towards an erogenous zone, is unbelievably sexy in itself. The best foreplay is about spending quality time, mutually building each other into such an aroused state that you are both ready for penetrative sex. But for those that love their statistics – the average time spent on foreplay is 14.4 minutes, while 16.2 minutes are spent on penetrative sex. I believe that in order to reach optimal arousal, you should be having at least fifteen minutes of fabulous foreplay.

It's in the Kiss

Ah, the beauty of a great kiss. So, what is it about kissing that makes us feel so good and why is it so important in foreplay? Well, the science of kissing is called philematology and it is believed that it is a learned behaviour rather than an instinctive one and its roots lie in the comfort that parents offered children in times of little food. It also has a lot to do with pheromones – the indefinable mix of pleasurable smells and sensations that we get when we kiss our partner (see pages 18–19). Kissing releases oxytocin (which encourages loving feelings); serotonin (which helps put you in a good mood) and dopamine (related to pleasure). No wonder kissing helps form an enduring chemistry within a relationship.

But the more basic truth is that we kiss because it makes us feel good and is one of life's greatest yet most simple pleasures. The lips and tongue are packed with ultra-sensitive nerve endings and kissing makes our blood pressure and our pulse rate increase, as well as our pupils dilate. All symptoms of the stimulation that we need for great sex.

Kissing our partner is also one of the most important ways of reinforcing bonding as well as a deeply intimate, personal and loving gesture. Whether it's a simple peck on the cheek or a full-on deep tongue kiss, it's the greatest expression of lust, love, closeness and joy that a relationship can have. It's also doing you a power of good – statistics have shown that people who kiss regularly have fewer sick days, fewer car accidents, live around five years longer than their non-kissing cousins and even earn 20–30% more than the non-kissers!

HIS AND HER SMOOCHING

There are intriguing differences between men and women when it comes to kissing.

A man's kiss . . .

- Is more often used as a means to an end – basically as a means of getting sex.
- Is used more frequently in reconciliation – they are more likely to literally kiss and make up.
- Is more likely to involve his tongue and develop into a full-on snog.
- Is a fickle thing – they are happy to have sex with someone who they consider to be a bad kisser or happy not to kiss at all before sex.

A woman's kiss . . .

- Is used as a mate selection technique – they subconsciously evaluate mating potential from the chemicals in a man's breath or saliva.
- Much more important throughout a relationship than it is for a man.

- Is used as much as a bonding gesture as a precursor to sex.
- Is a measure of the strength of her relationship – she can tell when the frequency or technique suddenly changes, perhaps indicating a possible waning of desire or attraction.

Types of kissing

Kissing is used throughout culture as a bonding and an emotional gesture. We kiss our friends hello and goodbye, kiss babies and kiss our family. But I want to take you through some of the kisses involved in sex, especially those used in foreplay.

The French kiss

We all know about the 'Frenchie' or the snog. This is also known as the soul kiss, because it is believed that the soul and its life travelled from one person to another through a breath, making its way across the tongues. The best way to French kiss is to gently brush your lips against your partner's mouth, while using your tongue to lick around their lips and then probe into his or her mouth with your tongue. They should respond in the same way and you can then take the tongue probing and exploration at a pace to suit you, upping your game and becoming faster and dropping back to more gentle mouth to mouth as the mood takes you. While the

French kiss was probably the first tongue locking, tonsil touching, mammoth kiss you ever shared with someone while you were at school, never underestimate the fabulousness of a French kiss. A fantastic snog gets your pulse racing, your knees trembling and your groin aching. Lips have the thinnest skin layer on the body and are packed with sensory neurons, which sends messages to the brain and body, transmitting sensory pleasure and affection which together combine to produce a massive natural high. In other words, a great snog can lead you to being hot and horny in a matter of seconds!

The roundabout kiss

Use the highly sensitive outer edges of your lips to gently trace along the outer edges of your partner's lips. Then run your tongue slowly along their upper and lower lip in a circling motion. Keep the pressure light and sensitive without letting your tongue slip into their mouth. It's erotic and very sensuous.

The waterfall kiss

This is one for the shower, the swimming pool, or even better the pouring rain. It's like a French kiss but wilder, using all that slippery water to literally drink in your partner's mouth and face.

The movie kiss

You know the one – often seen in Hollywood movies during the forties and fifties and on the front of Mills & Boon romances. The powerful kiss where the man pulls his partner in passionately and strongly with one hand firmly around her waist, while cradling the back of his partner's head with his other hand. He pulls her deeply into him and gives her a huge romantic, lip locked and commanding kiss.

The vacuum kiss

This playful kiss involves kissing open-mouthed, slightly sucking in as if you are drawing the air from your partner's mouth. This creates a vacuum that you can then release and reseal.

Lip-o-suction

This is a type of kiss in which the guy kisses the upper lip while the girl kisses his lower lip. Then they reverse. It's sensual and seductive.

Lip/neck nibble kiss

Pull in your partner's lower lip between your teeth, and suck or nibble gently. Or nibble and tease softly along their neck and then work your way up to their mouth.

The teasing kiss

Start kissing your partner gently, then more powerfully. Just as they are getting to enjoy it and expect more, pull back and just look them in the eye. It will drive them wild and make them want more . . .

The snake kiss

You use a gentle yet rapid flick of your tongue, all over your partner's lips, neck, nipples and belly button. Imagine you're a snake. This feels wonderful moving over the shaft of your lover's penis or round her labia (see Oral Sex, on page 85).

How to kiss like you mean it

We all have different tastes in kisses – some of us prefer deep, long, sensuous kisses. Others like gentle, tender nibbles or wild, frenzied passionate kissing. Whatever you like we will all have experienced that most awful of awful disappointments: the bad kisser. The man or woman who seems to storm in, locking their sloppy, stiff tongue on yours without any concern or sensitivity for whether you might be enjoying it too. Bad, insensitive kissers pay little attention to your own responses, so it doesn't take a genius to work out that they are unlikely to be a considerate, generous lover either.

So, while there is no exact formula for the perfect kiss, I reckon that this is a pretty good recipe, for a full-on erotic and sensual kiss, just right for foreplay, but do adapt it to your own preferences of course.

One of the most important ingredients to a fabulous kiss is to ensure that your breath smells fresh. Garlic breath is seriously off-putting – but chewing some parsley can help combat that, or simply request no garlic in your meal if you're going out to dinner. Unless you're snogging another smoker, smoker's breath can be pretty unpleasant too. Chewing gum (remember to remove it pre-snog!) or a small mint should mask any unpleasantness if you're not within brushing distance of toothpaste. Carry a small pack around with you. Drinking plenty of water, using a regular mouthwash, dental floss and a tongue scraper, can all keep your breath smelling sweet. If you think you might have bad breath, licking the back of your hand and then inhaling your saliva can be your best indicator to reach for the extra strong mints.

Practise snogging your hand. Yes, I know you probably last did this when you were in Juniors, but your hand – especially your palm – is a highly sensitive area and it's a great way to practise those tongue and mouth techniques. You can feel what tongue flicking, licking, nibbling and softly, barely rubbing your lips, or blowing gently, feels like when you do it to your own hand. Think about how all those different sensations might feel to your partner. While you might not kiss their mouth in the same way that you would kiss their vagina or penis – a whole different ball game, more of which later in this chapter – they will be thinking about your mouth exploring other areas. So you need to give a hint of the mood you're in – are you feeling confident, passionate and excited? Or sexy, sensual and slow? Show it with your mouth and tongue. This also works well with a new partner who probably won't know what you like or how to pace your early kisses.

Look your partner straight in the eye and take their face in both your hands. Keep your fingers open and let them slip tenderly towards the highly sensitive area, on their neck, just below their ears. Move your face oh-so slowly in towards them. Keep your jaw and your mouth relaxed and tilt your

head to one side. This avoids the passion-killer of the teeth-
or nose-bashing kiss, when you don't know which side your
partner is coming from.

With your lips just parted, cover your lover's mouth –
from the top and bottom lips, the corners and above and
below their mouth with light, delicate kisses. Keep these
gentle kisses going and then move down to their neck, and
work your way back up again. Move back to your partner's
mouth, but apply a little pressure with your mouth this time.
Use a little suck and nibble tug to their bottom lip, catching
it between your teeth. Keep this tender – the lips are not a
place to bite too hard.

Now, is the time to respond to your partner, who will be
getting more aroused now. You can start using your tongue
to tease them into using his or hers too. Flick your tongue
over and around your partner's lips before gently pushing it
into their mouth. The art is to keep moving your tongue
around your partner's, always responding to their pleasure
– as shown by their moans and groans of pleasure or the
way that they move their body or hands closer around your
face and body. The two cardinal sins of bad kissers are to
either keep an ironing-board straight, non-moving tongue
in your partner's mouth or moving it so wildly and
randomly, that it feels as if you are trying to excavate their
breakfast . . .

Basically, you carry on kissing in this way for as long as
the mood takes you – nibbling, licking, gentle biting and
tongue thrusting at a varying pace. How long is the perfect
kiss? Well the world record stands at just under 24 hours

(which took place in classically romantic Paris as it happens!) but the average length of a good snog is three and a half minutes. I reckon you need a least a couple of minutes to work steadily up to the fabulous finale, whether the kiss is just a kiss or a precursor to much more!

But what if, in spite of all this, your partner is an unresponsive kisser or just not doing it for you? Kissing is like a mini-version of sex itself, with all that lip and mouth foreplay before the penetration of the tongue itself. The tongue then mimics the penis, with all its thrusting at different speeds and different levels of passion. Just like making love you get considerate and inconsiderate kissers. Sensitive and insensitive kissers. Kissers who are too fast, too slow, too samey every time they kiss. So getting kissing right not only gives you an indication of what sex is going to be like, it excites, arouses and gives deep pleasure to you and your partner. So it's essential that you perfect your kissing technique (unless you both decide that it's not all that and there are other things that you prefer).

Ask your partner to kiss you the way they would want to be kissed. Make it fun and unpredictable and tell them you're going to judge them *X Factor* style. Then you're going to give them the perfect kiss and ask them to judge you. The actual act of kissing and reporting back can be sexy in itself, but most importantly it enables you to communicate with each other about what you want and is a whole lot easier than trying to describe in words what you want. 'Open your mouth more, put your tongue on the roof of my mouth, then waggle it around a bit' is not sexy talk . . .

It might seem a bit like a silly game and your partner might not remember every detail the next time you kiss, but it does mean that you both get what you want. And if either of you can't talk about how good kissing makes you feel and how you like it done, you've got zilch chance of tackling your mutual needs and desires during sex, which is a recipe for a dull, routine and ultimately unsatisfying sex life . . .

Talking Dirty

One of the important things to remember about talking dirty before or during sex is that it's not everyone's cup of tea. Some women find it demeaning or silly, some men just find it weird or don't know how to do it without causing offence or feeling ridiculous.

The point about dirty talk is that it's intimate, private and while it can be sexy to do with someone you hardly know, it works at its best when you're with someone you really trust. Like any other kind of foreplay, and less so than most, it should be used wisely. If you *have* to talk dirty every time just to get aroused then it's likely there's something wrong somewhere else in your sex life. It's better to use it sparingly, choosing the right moment and mood. Some men find that their erections can become a whimper at the mere suggestion that their partner wants them to fuck her harder. While for others, it's such a turn on, that they have to concentrate on the contours of the ceiling rose, in order not to ejaculate instantly!

For most women, unless they eff and blind on a regular basis, it's an opportunity to describe what they want during sex, in explicit, no-nonsense terms. In fact, the more 'virginal' and innocent you seem (or play act) the sexier it is. Words that would be out of place, unacceptable or deeply offensive in everyday conversation should be encouraged when you're talking dirty. They have quite a different meaning when having sex. However, some women do find words like bitch or slut demeaning, even used judiciously during sex, so if you're a guy that's turned on by this, approach with caution. If in doubt, slip in a gentle, naughty word and see how the land lies. Or keep to something sexy without being offensive or swearing. Keep it teasingly seductive rather than explicitly descriptive. Tell her that you want to pull her panties to one side and slip your fingers in, rather than calling her a dirty ho who needs a good seeing to!

And some guys feel uncomfortable and disrespectful using bad words. While others just can't bear to hear dirty words from their partner and it turns them off, rather than on. For some people, the cheesiness of dirty talk belongs in porn movies, not in the confines of their bedroom. Talking dirty, using taboo words, is your judgement call, but done well and used when the mood is right, it can be incredibly sexy, intense and powerful.

And dirty talk shouldn't just be reserved for sex. If your partner is working late, away for the night or just stuck in a boring meeting, send them a dirty text or email (just check the office policy on 'naughtiness' first!). Keep it simple – explain what you would like them to do to you when they get home, or tell them what you'd like to do to them. Explicit swear words work less well when written down. Better to simply describe that you're 'wearing nothing but stockings and a smile with a wet pussy' or that you're 'feeling horny and can't wait to be deep inside her'.

Touching

Touching is one of our earliest senses to develop. From the birth experience itself, to the first time our mother holds us or puts us to her breast through to the hugs and cuddles that we receive through early childhood that offer us security, love and comfort. Our skin is packed with sensory touch receptors that will give us different emotions from laughing when being tickled to passionate arousal when the foreplay is just right.

While there are some especially sensitive areas common to both men and women – fingertips, inner arms and thighs, for example – women have many more nerve endings in their skin than men and their skin tends to be softer and more delicate as well as less hairy, allowing the receptors to get the full-on treatment uninhibited by body hair! All this means that some men, if not particularly sensitive to touch themselves, do not understand the extreme pleasure that a woman feels to touch. Or they can get lazy about it, simply because they can't relate to how wonderful it can feel. So keep your hands as soft as possible. And your nails trimmed. While rough, calloused hands might be a feature of fantasy play, in truth they feel scratchy and unpleasant on tender skin.

Sex – as in penetrative sex – would be impossible without touch. Even if you're going in for the no-frills quickie on the stairs, moving from A to Z without any of the foreplay niceties described here, you can't actually manage this without some form of touch, even if it's just urgently grasping your partner towards you or guiding his penis into you as fast as time will allow . . .

Touch can take place just about anywhere on the body. Whether it's face, neck, mouth or ears. Breasts/chest or arms. Back and shoulders, inside and back of thighs, tummy, feet and the genitals of course. You get the picture.

As a general rule in foreplay, it's good to start touching the less sensitive areas of your partner's body and work your way up to the most sensitive. Some of this is pretty generic – most people's elbows are less sensitive than their genitals, of course – but learning about what pleases your partner (antennae ready for the moans, groans and positive responses) will teach you the unique hierarchy of sensitive spots that we all have. And however intimately you know your partner, there is something hugely sexy about pulling away from them, and spending some time just looking at their whole body, drinking in and feasting on those parts that you are going to touch and arouse very soon. And as much as you have learned to understand and appreciate your partner's – and your own – erogenous zones, it's also important to introduce variation and spontaneity into the places that you touch and the order in which you touch them. Touching in foreplay should not be like a set of instructions on a flat-pack piece of furniture, where there is only one way of assembling something to make a whole. Touching is about exploration and variation, however long you have been together as a couple. The human body is a complex and wondrous place, with highly sensitive and sexy areas that often get neglected. The inside of the arm and the back of the knee are wonderful places to touch (and kiss and lick . . .) but are often overlooked. In general the softer and more hair-free the skin, the more sensitive it is likely to be.

Massage

This can be an area of foreplay that people don't bother with for all sorts of reasons. Many think that if they haven't got a PhD in Swedish massage techniques then their hapless attempts may cause more pain than pleasure. Others think that it belongs in the realms of dodgy high-street massage parlours or in the unsexy bright lights of a professional chiropractor's clinic. Some people can't see why it even counts as foreplay, as it would appear to be a 'stand-alone' act, which takes too long to do properly anyway, rather than a precursor to sex itself.

Well the good news is that none of the above are reasons not to indulge in a little sensual massage. Like any form of foreplay it's simply how – rather than how long or how expertly – you do it that counts. And creating a little ambience or mood lighting along the way. True, it shouldn't be hurried – part of the pleasure is in the slow, sensual way in which you massage – but it's not a marathon of endurance either and doesn't require that every part of the body is given equal attention. Setting aside round an hour is a good start.

You need to set the mood. Turn off the overhead lighting (and your phone!) and use soft lamps or candle light instead. Make sure the room is warm, there's little more disappointing than shivering your way through a massage. Enjoy the silence, or play some atmospheric, slow music. Disco or heavy metal is not conducive to sensuality . . .

Sexy but simple massage techniques

While both of you should be undressed, sometimes it's good for a guy to keep a pair of close fitting underpants on, if he is giving a woman a massage, as a rock-hard penis can get in the way, position wise. Likewise it can be ultra sexy for a man if a woman keeps on a few clothes – bra, panties or just a pair of towering black patent heels.

A good massage is not about taking it in turns, at least not during the same session. If he is arousing you and unlocking all sorts of feelings and anticipation it can be a bit of passion killer to then have to swap places straight away!

Get your partner to lie face down on some soft towels. Flooring can be hard and nasty, give you carpet burns in some very uncomfortable places and no one wants to be worrying about oil stains on their precious Axminster while enjoying a carefree massage.

Warm some scented oil in the palms of your hands, ensuring that they are not too cold first! If you're adding concentrated essential oils to a plain base, use just a few drops or it can be too strong, both in terms of overwhelming smell as well as potentially burning the most sensitive parts of your skin.

Gently run your oiled fingertips down the length of your lover's back to get them used to the feel of your hands. Once they have relaxed use firmer strokes and a little more pressure. Use your hands in mirroring, symmetrical movements, using firm circular motions in and away from the backbone. Work your way down their back from the top to the bottom. Pay special attention to the shoulders, a firm but controlling massage here is an amazing stress reliever and relaxant.

When you reach the small of the back, start using your palms alone rather than your fingertips or whole hand. Push your flat palms firmly into the small of the back and work your way down to the lowest part of the buttocks. And then back up again. Lean over your partner to allow the weight of your body to give you control and strength.

You can turn your partner over at this point and pay attention to their chest or breasts, generally working your way from the top to the bottom. Go easy in terms of pressure on her breasts; they can be sensitive or painful, particularly just before or during her period. Or you can keep your partner on their front and carry on as before. You can be guided by your partner's moans of pleasure (if it's a moan of pain, ease up on the pressure) and verbal or non-verbal responses to what you are doing. Some people like to give a running commentary of when they want firmer or gentler strokes or where they want your hands to go, but although you are giving your partner a massage for their pleasure, part of the fun is that you are primarily in control. The important thing is to think of it in three more or less equal slices. The first 20 minutes or so should be spent in getting your partner relaxed, responsive and receptive. You should step it up a gear during the next 20 minutes, making it as sexy and as teasing as possible. Part of the pleasure of this part of the massage is the sweet almost trance-like anticipation of what's going to happen during the third part of this massage . . .

Genital massage: the ultimate hand job

Genital massage has been around for thousands of years and many of the most erotic and renowned books of their time like the *Kama Sutra* set a huge amount of importance to genital sex, believing it to be both sacred and tantric. As well as mind-blowingly pleasurable!

There are all sorts of techniques you can use to create the sublime genital massage and as men and women have pretty much different genitalia, I am going to give you a few variants specially designed for each other.

Male genital massage

For a woman giving her man a genital massage, there are a couple of techniques you can use. There's a soft, stroking rhythmical massage designed for the early stages of this last 20-minute slice of massage. Bend down or kneel so that you are between your man's legs. Use your fingers and thumb over his testicles in a gentle rolling motion. Then cup his testicles into the palm of your hands and use your fingers to softly stroke along the delicate and ultra sensitive skin of his scrotal sacs.

After that, hold the base of his penis firmly with one hand, while using the other to spiral and twist along the shaft of his penis along to the head. Slowly, as you work your way up, you will feel his erection stiffen and then use the palm and open fingers of your hand to rub back and forth and round and round over the head of his penis. Do this in a gentle but firm motion, without squeezing too tightly. The tip of his penis should feel gently wet, if not, use a little lubricant to make the sensation feel even hotter for him.

For a firmer version, and when your man is fully erect, open your hand so that your index finger and thumb are creating an 'O' shape. Firmly move your hand like this up and down the full shaft of his penis. Then create a 'V' shape between your index and middle finger, with your hand at an angle so that he can not only feel the tip of his penis pushing against and in and out of your fingers, but also feel the flat of your hand along the length of his penis. Working upwards, spiral your hand slightly so that all of his penis, rich in sensory nerve endings, gets the full delight of your attention.

While you can stop this massage at any time, either to try a little different foreplay or to have penetrative sex itself as the mood takes you, you can carry this right through to an almost certain orgasm for your man. By rubbing both hands up and down his penis, palms flat, and increasing speed and pressure, your rhythm will encourage him to orgasm. While you can give up with aching hands or wrists at any time during genital massage, this is not the best time to suddenly stop or even decrease pressure, because it's the very consistency of your massage that is building his excitement and to stop now, will probably feel pretty disappointing!

Female genital massage

If you're a guy wanting to give his woman a sensual massage, much the same 'rules' apply. Use a lubricant if necessary – not a scented oil. The vagina is far too delicate for anything perfumed. Once your partner is comfortable, with her legs flopped open, bend or kneel down so that your hands have free and full access to her body from the knees up to her breasts.

This is the part where you can both stimulate and slightly tease your partner. Starting at her inner legs, just near the knees use your palm and fingertips to brush gently along the contours of her inner thighs. Run your hands across and along all that delicious soft skin and feel her moans of pleasure. Use the back of your hand and fingers to create different levels of pressure and touch. Brush up and over her genitals, lightly touching and teasing as you move your hands upwards to her tummy, breasts and nipples. Keep brushing with your palms, fingertips and back of your hand to create a varied but rhythmical sensation.

Gradually, bring your hand down towards her vagina and using your index finger, in a circular motion, gently 'paint' a circle on and around the lips (the outer labia) of her vagina. You will sense her arousal and anticipation in a number of ways. Her breathing may quicken, she may moan, groan or sigh, shift in position to encourage you to go further or just express this verbally. She will also start to feel moist and warm and you may see her labia glisten. Just like your penis, the labia are full of nerve endings and so the blood stream is near the surface. Her labia may start to deepen in colour as the stimulation sends the blood to the surface of the skin.

Using the palm of your hand and a little more pressure, to knead the labia in an up and down motion, back and forth from her anus to her vagina. This is the point to begin to touch her clitoris, with your index or middle finger. Massage or roll your finger gently over her clitoris – don't squeeze, pinch or press her clitoris. This is the most sensitive part of a woman's vagina and there can be a fine line between extreme pleasure and intense pain!

If this is making her feel good her breathing will have quickened, her moans become more vocal and her body will writhe more, and her legs will open wider, to encourage you to carry on.

If she is enjoying the clitoral stimulation use your index finger to circle her clitoris, with ever increasing rhythmical pressure. If this seems too sensitive for her – and you'll know by her reaction, so don't be alarmed – go back to making circular palm movements across her inner and outer labia instead.

Hopefully, her writhing, breathing, moans and direct instruction will show you that she's reaching a peak of arousal where she's ready to orgasm. She may be well-lubricated at this point, or you may need to use a little extra lubrication, so gently push a finger or two into her vagina, with your fingertips upwards, as if you are reaching for her tummy from inside. You may feel her G-spot under your fingertips. It's a fairly unmistakeable raised area with a slightly ridged texture. As you feel her further arousal, gently but firmly pull her towards you from within, with a beckoning type gesture. If you can manage to use your other hand to continue to circle her clitoris with your finger, you are likely to have a very happy and fulfilled orgasmic lover on your hands. Literally!

So, I can sense you asking, isn't this massage business, especially genital massage, just another way of describing a hand job? Well, to a degree it's much the same sort of techniques and has the same desired effect. The point about the massage is that it's the third part, the denouement or culmination if you like, of a longer, sensuous, body massage. But like any good foreplay session, there are no strict instructions about where one technique stops and another begins. It's not a prescriptive science and what starts as massage may end in oral sex, or whatever tickles your fancy. This is about spontaneity, pleasure, and arousal and above all fun. Any 'rules' are all yours for the making and breaking . . . So yes, it *is* a pretty good way of giving a fabulous hand job.

Hand Jobs

Not an especially lovely term for something that gives men and women such great pleasure. But as well as using it as an important element of your foreplay repertoire, it's fun at other times too. It's great if you just want to use hand jobs for a while until you're ready for sex with a new partner – or even if you're not ready for oral sex yet. Maybe you're still a virgin and don't want to have sex for the first time until you feel ready. Perfecting giving great 'hand' will get you prepared and ready in the nicest possible way.

You might want to try it in public – it's exciting, naughty and you're much less likely to get caught or get into trouble if you do get found out! Try some 'hands on' sex in a quiet part of the park on a sunny day. Or in the dark, at the movies. It beats snogging in the back row for excitement value! Or try it under a blanket on a plane. Learning to be discreet and quiet is all part of the game.

Or give a hand job while you're kissing your partner. Having the deliciousness of a seriously sexy snog, while having his fingers probing your vagina or running her hand along the ever-stiffening shaft of your penis can feel ultra sensational.

Other ways of giving him a 'hand job'

So because of time or inclination, you're not going for the full-on massage, but you want to perfect your hand-job technique, give him ultimate pleasure and save yourself the distracting repetitive strain injury of an aching wrist during the process. And if you haven't got a clue as to what you should be doing or are scared of hurting your partner, most men are delighted to explain in explicit detail exactly what would make them feel good. After all, he is likely to have been masturbating since he was a lad and will know the ins and outs of his own version of penis pleasure better than almost anything else in the world. And although you may like your hand stimulation done slowly and softly, men generally like theirs faster and harder. If you remember nothing else, keep a firm, confident, moist grip and build up the rhythm as your partner becomes more aroused.

And I know this might sound bonkers, but practising on a simple vibrator is a good idea. Or even a carrot or an unripe banana. No one is going to see you doing it and it helps create the fist/finger technique that men are so grateful for. Always use a strong, upwards motion, twisting your hand more as your reach the top of the vibrator (or carrot!). Spend about five seconds on each upward movement, getting gradually faster over a few minutes, while using a much swifter and firmer pumping action as you draw your hand back down to the base. This is the simplest sort of hand job and is highly effective stuff when used on the real thing . . .

Even if he seems to have a lot of clear fluid at the end of his penis – in scientific terms this is known as pre-ejaculatory fluid and varies from man to man and occasion to occasion – it's worth keeping some lubricant handy. Dry palms, or even nervous sweaty ones, will always feel like a dream to a man who will simply adore a hand job from you but wet slippery hands will take him to heaven. Do bear in mind that the head of an uncircumcised penis tends to be more sensitive, so be mindful of the foreskin and the frenulum – the little stringy bit between the head and the shaft of the penis. The shaft can take a fair battering, but the head of the penis is quite another thing. Remind yourself of how sensitive your clitoris can be and apply the same rule,

And get yourself in a comfortable position. Part of giving a great hand job is to be relaxed. Lying by his side, twisting your hands into position will give you wrist and arm ache, so sit astride his chest. Or get him to kneel on the bed, facing you, so you get down to it in the most comfortable position for you. And if you're right-handed, it makes sense to start with that hand, your stronger hand. And vice versa of course.

Note how I've used the word 'hand job' in inverted commas in the heading of this section. That's because one of the best ways of giving your man a hand-job hardly involves your hands at all. Squeeze some lubricant between your breasts and lift them together (this is where your hands do come in useful!) to create a deep cleavage. Then let your man lean over you and thrust in and out of this lovely warm, soft and wet 'faux' vagina. He'll love it. There he is in a position of manly power, riding over you with his penis thrusting oh-so close to your face in one of your hottest erogenous zones. It will feel naughty and exciting and letting him ejaculate like this will make him eternally grateful for the pleasure.

Or you could clasp your fingers and hands together as if you were praying and then slide his penis through the gap between your hands. You can use your thumbs and fists to create different pressure and slide your hand up and down the shaft of his penis, twisting them from side to side as you go up and down. You can also use your hands to create a basket weaving, twirling effect over the tip of his penis and then slide your hands back up and down his shaft again, at whatever speed is pleasing you both. As with all form of hand jobs, some lubricant will always make it feel better for both of you. And swapping hands, due to wrist ache, is quite acceptable, especially if you keep the rhythm going while you swap from right to left.

Rhythm in all hand jobs and genital massage is key. While his penis might not be quite as sensitive as your vagina, going too slowly gets a little dull and might not make him feel as aroused as he'd like. While going too fast can make him sore and oversensitive. Just like any other foreplay technique, start off slowly and then build to a faster rhythm as he nears climax.

Oh and a last word regarding climax. Most hand jobs – but not all, it's not obligatory – will lead to your man coming to orgasm or climax. Semen can be sticky and faintly smelly. It can have the texture of lumpy wallpaper paste. And it goes cold and claggy very quickly. While it might not have the texture or taste (more of which later) of molten chocolate, and it's undeniable messy, especially when it leaves a wet patch on the sheets or gets stuck in your hair or on your face, don't complain about the clean up process. It doesn't add to the sensuality and excitement of the moment. A fuss-free wipe with a tissue is all that's needed. And however firmly and masterfully you bring your man to orgasm, the moment he has climaxed his penis will suddenly become ultra-sensitive and limp. This can look incredibly cute and you might be tempted to give it a little more oral stimulation, because of this or the fact that you're (rightly) proud to have brought your man to such a pleasurable climax. But beware, it's probably best to let sleeping dogs lie during this recovery period, which can take up to an hour or more to desensitise once again.

Pushing a finger into a guy's rectum, especially when close to orgasm, can seriously spice things up. Some men don't like it, as they think it has gay connotations – slightly mad as their sexy woman's finger up their bottom is unlikely to get them to change their sexuality. If in doubt, run your finger around the rim of his anus and see what reaction you get. A clenched bum or a seismic shift in position isn't a great sign. But if you can feel him yield a little and push his bottom further towards your finger, insert your index finger gently but firmly into his bottom, keeping your palm face up (towards his tummy) and use a beckoning gesture with your finger. You may touch his prostate gland, a few inches in. Don't worry it doesn't feel especially odd. This is also known as the male G-spot and for many men, hitting this ultra-sensitive part of his inner bum will make him climax faster than almost anything else. Remember to use plenty of lubrication – this is a very dry area – and keep your fingernails short. The skin is pretty tough in there, but he needs to feel your fingertips, not your inch-long acrylic falsies!

Having said that most guys like most women giving them a hand job, the most common whinge that men make about them is all to do with rhythm. Ask him how it feels, to gauge the right pressure and speed. Smooth, confident rhythm (even if this is your first time) always goes down well. Jerky, stop–start movements, swapping hands too slowly, numb fingers and obviously aching wrists as well as too much time being spent on the lovely hard bit at the bottom of his shaft, rather than the much more sensitive head end of the penis are also common complaints. It doesn't have to be spectacularly complicated or an Olympic sport – but remembering the rhythm rule is always good.

Other ways of giving her a hand job

Don't get too conceited here guys, but the truth is you're probably better at giving her a hand job than she is at giving you one. This is not because you're more in tune with a woman's body, but because you've probably spent a considerable part of your adolescence and early adulthood trying to get into a girl's knickers or persuade her to have sex with you and you are familiar with the 'means to an end' aspect of giving great hand. Well, we're still talking means to an end – but this time it's to bring your lover to an orgasm, not just so as you can get from A to Bed in the fastest possible time!

The genital massage techniques listed on page 71 are amongst the best ways of stimulating a woman, but these other methods are also pretty useful to add to your repertoire. As with so many foreplay techniques, variety is important in keeping your sex life hot – routine is what makes women quietly seethe. Also, women vary hugely in the sensitivity levels of their vaginas, especially around or on the clitoris and pleasure can give way to pain at a moment's notice. Don't let that put you off, you'll soon hear her moans change or feel her pull back if you have gone in too deep or inserted one finger too many. And it's always better to use a lubricant, especially if you're starting from 'cold' rather than a lengthy massage session.

It's worth remembering that although you and your penile best pal have been intimate with each other since early childhood, many women don't masturbate and therefore don't know what the insides of their vagina actually feels like. Many haven't even seen it – never having placed a mirror between their legs to investigate in any detail. So go easy on her – especially if she is less familiar with her vagina than you are! On the plus side, even the tightest of vaginas widens and lengthens enough to allow a finger or two inside comfortably, but do make sure you've built up to this kind of penetration with other foreplay first. Women take longer to arouse than a man and with lack of arousal comes lack of moisture and elasticity.

Be aware of the build up that your partner needs. Try brushing her inner thighs with your fingers and the back of your hand in a swishing motion, carefully moving upwards towards her vagina. Pay special attention to her highly erogenous zones of neck, breasts and anywhere else she is especially partial to. She is likely to open her legs wider as she wills you to touch her genitals. Tease her for a little longer – make her want you even more as she becomes increasingly aroused. Try pressing your palm and closed fingers against her vagina and she'll give you plenty of indication of what she wants and where, by pushing and grinding her vagina towards your hand. She might squeeze her thighs tightly together; to clasp your hand between them to increase some of the intensity. Just leave your hand there and let her do most of the work against your hand. Don't panic if she doesn't feel wet – not all women do. Try testing how moist she is by gently probing your middle fingertip inside her vagina. She may well feel wetter in there, so use that to moisten her around the labia with that finger. Or use a little lubrication – or even your saliva. But don't spit into your palm and then slap your hand 'down there'. It's annoying, insulting and very unsexy!

Try squeezing your index and middle fingers together and stroke the outer lips of her vagina. Move them rhythmically from side to side, sweeping right over her vagina, getting faster as she becomes wet and aroused. Slide them into her vagina and carry on with gentle but rapid rocking movements, probing and thrusting a little deeper every few strokes. This mimics intercourse itself and depending on her arousal levels, and the size and depth of her vagina (and the dimensions of your fingers!) she might open enough to allow you to insert your ring finger too. Don't be too hasty to do this – or indeed any hand-job technique – as the sensitivity factor can kick in pretty quickly in this delicate part of her body.

You can also use your index and middle fingertips to work around the inside edges of her vagina, making tiny circular movements as you work your way around. This is a highly erogenous area, and is often overlooked during foreplay, yet it often excites a woman relatively quickly yet avoids direct stimulation of the clitoris that some women find just too sensitive.

Leaving her panties on is another way of being very sexy with your fingers. Build up to this by stroking her breasts, nibbling, licking and touching the bits she likes best first. Then let your hand drift down to her knickers. If you've played your part well, the crotch of her pants should feel a little damp. Run your fingers along the edges of the crotch and let your fingers gently brush against her vagina, over the outside of her pants. Then gently tease her pants to one side and let your fingers start playing with the warm, yielding flesh of the labia and vagina itself. This is a hot and sexy way to start off whatever hand technique you choose, as she'll be primed and ready for your fingers to explore further.

And give a little thought as to how women masturbate. There tends to be more clitoral stimulation than thrusting of their own fingers or vibrators, so just shoving a finger or two in there and hoping for the best is not the way to go. Always use clitoral stimulation – around or on the clitoris, depending on how sensitive she is – together with those magic fingers. Keep it regular, slow and gentle. Women do not like rushed, rough men playing with the most delicate and sensitive part of their body. Listen to what her body is saying and watch for stop/go signs. Women are all different; we don't masturbate as much as you and we're not as familiar with our genitals as you are. Hey, they're not even on the outside of our bodies. She may be quiet, she may be noisy but if she's opening her legs wider and pressing herself against you, read that as a positive sign. If she pulls away from you, clenches her vaginal muscles or makes a sudden jerky movement, you are probably being too rough. Remember that the female orgasm lasts much longer than the male climax. It might seem strange, but our orgasms last three or four times longer than yours. We build to a peak, stay there for a little and then subside gently – rather than one explosive rush. So *please* don't stop what you're doing while we're still having an orgasm – it's just not the same!

Oral Sex

The simple truth is, that almost everybody – men and women – love to receive great oral sex. For some people it ranks even higher than penetrative sex itself. There is something exciting, intimate and sensual about using your tongue and mouth to stimulate your partner's genitals.

Done well, it's an immensely generous part of foreplay. You are literally dedicating yourself to giving your partner a mind-blowing orgasm. Taking time and care and lavishing attention on your partner are incredibly important. Finding it distasteful, being picky or doing it through obligation are absolute killers to oral sex. And yet, it's also a hugely powerful performance, where you, the giver, are in absolute control. It is one of the most erotic and important parts of foreplay. And yet, there is much confusion over how to do it, whether you are doing it 'right' or whether your partner enjoys it.

A blow-by-blow technique for her

There's an old joke that you maybe have heard. Why was the bride wearing a smile when she walked down the aisle?

Because she knew she'd given her last blow job. And therein lies part of the problem. Women often don't like giving blow jobs to their man because of the 'yeuch' factor, because it's tiring and feels like hard work, they get concerned about gagging and especially because they really don't want to run the risk of their partner ejaculating into their mouth. The good news is that you do *not* have to swallow if you don't like the taste, texture or sensation of semen. You can give great head and then either pull back your mouth from his penis and let him ejaculate over your breasts or elsewhere on your body or simply use it as a foreplay method, before you have actual penetrative sexual intercourse. But bear in mind that he will really want to ejaculate into your mouth. Sure, semen is a bit gloopy and can vary in taste depending on what he's eaten, but there's not as much of it as you might think, you can swallow it quickly (like medicine) and it's got an earthy flavour, rather than a disgusting taste. You can even keep it in your mouth and then spit it discreetly into your hand or a tissue, once you're done. Anything, so long as you don't make a face and declare it to be the most revolting thing you have ever tasted!

Giving oral sex should never feel like a duty or an obligation. Or the price you pay for keeping your man interested. Or what you have to do, in order to procure that golden bauble you saw in the high-street jeweller's and your birthday is coming up fast. So, it figures that you're going to need to hone up on the techniques that make him feel oh-so good as well as learning to love the power it gives you and the pleasure it gives him.

Whatever position you choose, it's always better to wait until your lover is almost fully erect before putting his penis into your mouth. And it won't always respond as you expect. Don't worry, it's unlikely to be your technique – it will probably be due to tiredness, stress or drinking too much.

Before I go onto the technical detail of giving your man fabulous oral sex, it's worth bearing in mind the few no-nos that can turn any pleasure into pain or disappointment. Keep your teeth well back from your lips – biting his penis is not a good feeling for him. If you're in any doubt about what you're doing, keep it firm but gentle, rhythmical and make him feel like you're doing it for pleasure, not duty. Or simply ask him what he wants and how he likes it. Communication in sex – especially the more intimate variety – is vital to success and fulfilment.

I am going to keep this easy and straightforward. Using the eight suggested stages below, you will give your man the most amazing pleasure, while learning a little about how and why that pleasure is so much in the power of your hands, mouth and tongue.

1. Suggest that he keeps his pubic hair closely trimmed. Preferably not shaved, however, as stubble rash is not attractive and doesn't feel at all good. And picking bits of pubic hair from your mouth (or worse, coughing them up!) is both distracting and not very sexy. Make your man aware that he needs to keep up good standards of hygiene and encourage him to wash his genitals first. A penis smelling of pee is not a great start to

what should be a hugely enjoyable experience for both of you.

2. Don't just dive in and grab his penis as if it's a gear stick or sword that you're about to swallow, even though it tends to move and jerk with some very odd-seeming movements, as it becomes erect. Build up his anticipation and tease him a little first. Kiss him and then work your way down his body using your hands, mouth and tongue to nibble, stroke, lick and turn him on. Concentrate on his erogenous zones – his neck, nipples and the area just above and around his genitals, including his inner thighs.

3. Move back up from his inner thighs and cup his testicles in your hand, licking them both with large swirling movements, as if you're tasting the most delicious sweetmeats in the world. Then – and this is the killer move – cradle his penis in your hands and take a long, lingering, lustful look at it. Then do the same look, but directly into his eyes. This will drive him wild with impatience. Keeping direct eye contact while actually giving him a blow job will also add to his excitement. If in any doubt about this, check out a couple of soft porn movies and just watch the way those oh-so grateful girls look their partner straight in the eye.

4. Slide your hand up and over his penis, pulling the foreskin so it slides up and over the head of his penis. Keep lubricant within easy reach at this stage, you want your hands to feel as slippery as possible. Before you actually draw his penis into your mouth – using one or both hands to steady it into place – create saliva in your

mouth so that you can maximise the moisture on his penis. Drink some water if you need to.

5. Lower your mouth and lick all along the shaft of his penis, from the bottom to the top. One direct, straight lick is all you need to do before swooping your mouth straight over his erect penis, taking it in as deeply as is comfortable. Many women feel a gag reflex when their lover's penis goes in too deeply into their throat, but be reassured he'll still have enormous pleasure even if you can only take it part of the way in. Grip the bottom of the shaft of his penis, alternating moving your hand up and down with your mouth sliding up and down over his penis. Maintain a good and regular rhythm, swirling your hands and mouth and make sure you lick right around the rim of the head of his penis as well as playfully licking his frenulum, the stringy bit under his penis, plus the perineum, the highly sensitive area between his penis and his testicles.

6. Keep the rhythm regular and confident, concentrating on his penis and savouring every moment. Your teeth can get in the way (and you'll soon know if you've nibbled into him!) so push your lips over your gums as much as possible. From time to time give him direct eye contact too as you groan and 'mmmm' with eagerness, joy and pleasure. Some men like to push your head down hard on their erect penis and while some women don't mind this, it can also take his penis in too far, so feel free to push his hand away if he attempts this porn star type manoeuvre. The head of his penis is much

more sensitive than the shaft, so you can happily spend more time there, than worry about 'deep throating'.

7. As you sense that he is ejaculating – and don't be afraid to ask him to let you know, men enjoy being very vocal at this moment, announcing to the world in no uncertain terms that they are coming with an 'ohmygod' or two – you can choose to swallow, pull his penis to your breasts or tummy or finish off with penetrative sex. If you need more straightforward signs of imminent ejaculation, or your man is less vocal, his penis is likely to swell and go a darker red and his testicles will seem to shrink into his body.

8. A final word about the post finale. If he has ejaculated during oral sex, then his penis will shrink into a dear little fellow, nestling on his tummy. While we have masses of oxytocin, the cuddle hormone, coursing through our bodies at this stage, your man will probably just want to crash out. Don't be offended by this – it's not indifference, just different hormones. And his penis, cute as it may look, will be very sensitive so avoid direct touch at this stage – though a little kiss is nice to seal the deal.

Positions

Positions for giving a blow job to your man are not quite as varied or as important as the other way around, because it simply doesn't tend to last as long. While women might need oral sex to orgasm at all, men tend to see it as a prelude to sex (albeit a hugely enjoyable one) and he might want to save his ejaculation for penetrative sex itself.

The classic position is for your man to lie on his back while you work your way down to his penis, eventually settling, face down, between his thighs. You can use your hands and your mouth to control the process. You're also in a fabulous position to give him that direct eye-to-eye contact, as you look up while his penis is sliding deeper into your mouth.

But it's also exciting if he stands at the end of the bed and you sit or lie facing him. It gives your hands and mouth control over his whole genital area and means you can also turn over and lick underneath him, giving his testicles and perineum full attention.

The other position, which men love because it seems submissive for the woman, is for him to stand while you kneel down in front of him. There is nothing wrong with a little agreed submission (or domination) in oral sex, just beware of carpet burns to your knees if you're down there too long! Men tend to favour this position, not just because it seems submissive for the woman, making them seem more powerful, but also because it looks like you are worshipping at the altar of his most prized possession!

A blow-by-blow technique for him

There is a certain misguided squeamishness associated with oral sex, especially from the male point of view. Let me just get this straight: the vagina is a self-cleansing organ, it doesn't need washing out or douching and while it remains primarily inside the body it is naturally fresh and musky smelling and often a lot cleaner than a man's penis, which spends a lot of time stuffed into close-fitting pants, trouser crotches and jeans that might have benefited from more regular visits to the dry-cleaners! Provided your woman adopts basic hygiene principles – having a daily shower and keeping her pubic hair closely trimmed – there really is nothing not to like! And guys who give great oral sex rarely lack a partner.

Women all taste slightly different and even your own long-term partner's taste will vary according to what she has eaten (spicy food and garlic are the worst 'offenders') or drunk, her time in the menstrual cycle and if she is taking any medication. It's an essential part of foreplay and fulfilling a woman and is a technique that needs to be learned and understood as well as possible. However, if you still feel slightly squeamish (shame on you!), gently washing your partner's genitals with a warm, clean face flannel can actually feel quite sexy and might help your own inhibitions. Or have a little fun in the shower or bath together before you get down to it. And please don't give up on us before we have had our orgasm. It can take a while for us to come and our climaxes last much longer than yours. Even if you think it's all over, keep going with a strong and uninterrupted rhythm until you get a signal to withdraw. Just like your penis, the clitoris gets very sensitive post-orgasm, so she'll probably pull back when the show's over.

So, given that women generally love receiving oral sex and

it would be an absolute dereliction of duty to leave it out of your repertoire, and you so should *not* wait to be asked, here are my top five suggestions to take her orally induced orgasm to a mind-blowing level.

1. Suggest that she trims her pubic hair closely, especially around her outer labia. Pubic hair can trap the smells of day-to-day life and even the freshest smelling just-stepped-out-of-the-shower vagina can lose its sweetness as the day goes on. And picking bits of pubic hair from your mouth or wiping your mouth on your hand is both distracting and not very sexy.

2. Tease her a little and build up her anticipation. Don't dive under the covers and head straight for the target – you are not a Spitfire on a bombing mission! Start at her mouth and work your way down her body, using your mouth and hands to touch, lick, nibble and kiss all the way down. Pay lots of attention to her erogenous zones – breasts and nipples, tummy and inner thighs. You want her to be nice and wet and already turned on by the time you arrive at her vagina. Her hips will probably be thrusting upwards by now, aching you to explore her with your tongue. Take a moment to pull back and take a long, look at her lovely vagina. Look at how beautiful it is, lust after it and tell her your appreciation of its beauty. This is a massive turn-on for women who rarely get to see what their genitals actually look like and if they do, see a mirrored, angled reflection of something that can seem to them to be anything

but beautiful! Your enthusiasm and devotion is seriously sexy in itself.

3. Use the whole of your tongue, not just the tip. Using the flat, wide part of your tongue in confident, slow and sweeping movements is much more erotic than tentatively waggling the tense tip of your tongue about at random. Using side-to-side strokes with your mouth and tongue will ensure that you don't over stimulate one area only or make the clitoris overly sensitive.

4. Part her labia with your fingers and stroke slowly and gently around the clitoral area. Using the relaxed, flat of your tongue, circle around the clitoris and then let those slow, lazy but strong movements drift around the whole area of the vagina, lapping firmly, but roughly, and drinking in her juices. Some women like the feeling of sucking, rather than just licking, but others find this too intense so take your cue from her body language responses. If she pushes in towards you, enabling her to position herself higher and deeper, this definitely indicates you are pushing the right pleasure buttons. Wriggling and pulling back, might mean that she's not enjoying it quite so much. She might also use more direct words like 'deeper', 'harder' or 'that's amazing'. Keep it slow, gentle and consistent. And be patient – it can take some women up to half an hour to have an orgasm, although many are much quicker than this.

5. Open your fingers spread your hands wide and pull her bottom firmly (if this was a Mills & Boon novel, I'd be tempted to say 'masterfully') towards you. Keep your

tongue moving in a wide, confident circle, covering as much area as possible, but also let your tongue stray towards her anus – a highly sensitive area. Don't be tempted to give up or pull away at this stage. If you're doing a good job, she will be having an amazing time and may well be on her way to her climax. Some women move a lot during this period, gyrating and stretching to enjoy every moment, while others lie still, concentrating on and savouring every sensation. Inserting a finger or two into her as she's about to come can also give her the deep thrusting that some women need at this stage. Or stiffen and roll your tongue making it into a faux penis and use this to thrust into her deeply. But bear in mind that a lot of women do *not* need penetrative sex, whether a finger, your tense tongue or your penis to reach an orgasm.

Positions

So now you know the basics of oral-sex techniques, let's look at some of the best positions for getting down there.

The classic position is one of the best, as she can see what's going on and you're supporting her too. Let her lie on the bed while you kneel between her legs and then lift her legs over your shoulders, letting them rest there. She can use her shoulders and hands to support herself and adjust her position. You could also try lying flat on your tummy, with your head between her legs. She can reach down and cradle your head towards her or lift her bottom in the air to direct you further.

The other classic position is the 69er, where you 'top to tail' to give pleasure to each other simultaneously. One of the best-known positions, it can be doubly exciting. But in reality, it is actually quite difficult to concentrate on the matter in hand (or mouth!) when you are being sent to heaven by being given an amazing blow job by your partner! Plus oral sex isn't about giving turns – although consistent one way pleasuring is poor bedroom etiquette – it's about being generous, considerate and sexually attentive to your partner. Having simultaneous blow jobs can be a bit emotionally and sexually draining, especially at a time when you want to savour every moment of the giving – or receiving – process.

One of the most exciting positions for her, because it gives her sublime control, is for you to lie face up on the bed, while she climbs on top of you facing the bed head or wall. She then lowers herself onto your face, using the wall or bed head for support. Using her knees and hands she can lift herself up and away from your mouth if it all gets a bit intense, or lower herself further onto your mouth and tongue, indicating that she'd like more pressure.

Another great position is for your lover to get down on all fours, supporting her body weight on her hands and knees. She could be facing you, in which case you can slide underneath her, using a cushion or pillow to support your head and get it to the right position, without giving you neck cramp. Or she could be facing away from you and you can lick and taste her from behind.

It's also very erotic to lick her while she's wearing her sexy panties. Licking through soft, delicate fabrics like lace, silk or satin can make her highly aroused. If you then tease away the crotch of her knickers with your fingers before pushing your tongue into her, she's going to go through the roof sexually speaking.

Hopefully, much of the above will have given you some serious food for foreplay thought, so let's move onto the business of penetrative sex and the delicious variety that lies in store . . .

4 Positions: the Best Five Basics

Five basic positions? There will be some of you out there who will think 'Only five? I can achieve more than that in just one night'. Others will try to imagine what those five might be. The vast majority of people will pretty much know something about all of them, have tried a few, but – especially if in a long-term or not highly sexually active relationship – are used to the missionary position, with the man on top, most of the time, with the occasional shift of position to one of the others. The truth is that most people only make love in three different positions, ever, throughout the whole of their sexually active life.

I am not suggesting that you should turn yourself overnight into a sexual athlete. This book is about pleasure and enjoyment not about racing through the entire sexual repertoire from A–Z, setting records or proving anything to anyone – including yourself or your lover. But given that the vast majority of couples in a successful relationship need regular sex to enable their relationship to thrive and that one of the most common reasons for the breakdown of a relationship is a lack of intimacy due to predictability and boredom, it stands to reason that a relationship where you simply have sex on a Sunday morning in the missionary position only is going to run out of steam sooner or later. And although these five basic positions form the cornerstone of fun and pleasurable sex, without the need for toys or fancy equipment, role-play style dressing up or the supple body of a Grand Master in Tantric Yoga, there is a massive dearth of available information on the five basic positions for having sex. So why is that?

- Sexperts write much less about these five positions than almost any other area of sex. Foreplay and fancy sexual techniques are considered to be much more entertaining.
- The majority of women can't orgasm through penetrative sex alone. So it stands to reason that books and magazine articles devote considerably more time to non-penetrative sex, including oral sex and the A-, G- and U-spots.
- Intercourse itself is considered to be the most obvious aspect of the sex act and so it's neglected in favour of writing about what people might not know.

So understanding the basic positions – the whistles and bells come in the next chapter – is pretty critical to making and sustaining an intimate relationship. Even if you keep your sexual repertoire to regular lovemaking just using these basic five positions, you will actually give yourself a massive advantage in keeping your relationship together – as well as having a fabulous time in the process.

Man on top: missionary position

The missionary position is the most conventional, traditional and favoured position for couples in a new relationship and those who have been together a long while. Its rather odd name apparently derives from the fact that when the early European missionaries were sent out to 'tame' the 'wild and excessive' indigenous population (who were propagating the species in all sort of unorthodox positions) these missionaries considered making love with the man on top to be the most acceptable position to adopt in the eyes of God. Ironic really, given that up until then, the people of the colonies were probably not only having an amazing time enjoying sex in all sorts of positions, many of them were happily indulging in the very same *Kama Sutra* positions that so many people want to know about today.

The missionary position does allow a special feeling of intimacy between you and your partner and is easy to do in the comfort of your bedroom. You can kiss, touch and have direct eye contact throughout this position. It is comfortable for both partners, requires little imagination or effort for a woman and hits the mark in a functional sort of way. There is absolutely nothing *not* to like about the missionary position, so please don't think you have to ever consider banishing this from your repertoire just because it is the most conventional position. Although, banning it for a while – for deliberate reasons – means that you'll have to try and expand your sexual repertoire, which is exciting in its own way. Used on its own – like any other position – doing it missionary style can get predictable and boring – and let's face it, we women don't have to make a great deal of effort with our guy on top. So let's give him a break, a bit of a rest and show him what else you can do as well!

Having said that, we're probably all going to do the missionary position at least as often as any other position, so let's look at how to do it properly and what works in its favour, sexually speaking, and what doesn't.

Essentially, in its most uncomplicated form the missionary position involves the woman lying flat on her back with her legs spread flat out, pulled up towards her chest or wrapped around her partner. A woman can wrap one or both of her legs around her man in a number of different ways – she can wrap her legs around the back of her partner's legs, around his bottom or his back, or over his shoulders. The higher a woman lifts her legs, the deeper the penetration will be.

The man lies face down on top of the woman, usually with his legs between hers, with his penis in the right position to directly penetrate her vagina. A woman can arch her back or use a cushion or a pillow underneath her bottom or in the small of her back, to raise her pelvis allowing for easier and deeper penetration. A woman can also squeeze her thighs together, with a man's legs outside hers, to get more clitoral stimulation.

So that was the rather unsexy descriptive part. What are the positives and negatives of missionary position sex?

Man on top – the ins

- It's comfortable and easy for both partners.
- Penetration varies due to the positioning of the woman's legs and how strongly the man thrusts.
- When we lust after someone, it's the first position that we think about when we want to have sex.
- If we women are feeling self-conscious about our wobbly bits, lying on our backs spreads the flab and gives us a flatter tummy.
- It's a great position if you're feeling in that lazy I-fancy-sex mood, but are not climbing the walls with unrequited desire.
- You can indulge in full and direct eye contact and there is a lot of skin-to-skin contact.
- You can talk and kiss throughout sex, which makes it more romantic.
- Men like the control it gives them and some women enjoy the passive position of having the man do most of the work as it lets them reach climax more easily, due to the fact that they don't have to concentrate on what they are doing!
- If a man is prone to premature ejaculation, the fact that he is more in control of his thrusting can help him hold off an orgasm for longer.

Man on top – the outs

- As it's the most conventional and commonplace position, it can get predictable and boring if there isn't some other sexual variation.

- It's difficult for women to move around much, so she feels she has less control.
- You can't see much of the real action going on during penetration and that can diminish excitement.
- A big or heavy man on top of a woman can feel a bit constricting and uncomfortable.
- Given that (at least) two thirds of women need clitoral stimulation to orgasm means that the vast majority of women won't climax by the basic missionary position alone.
- A man can get tired supporting most of his weight on his arms.

Woman on top – the cowgirl

Now this is more like it! For a woman, being on top can feel exciting, liberating and powerful. A woman has entire control over the depth, pace and angle of sex. She also allows her man to have a rest, while she gets on with the work. Men adore this, because they love the feeling of being ridden – hence the cowgirl name. This position is also known as the reverse missionary.

The basic version of the woman on top position is for the man to lie flat on his back, while the woman sits astride him. She should bend her knees and get into a kneeling position while she lowers herself onto his erect penis. With the woman in this position, she can control vaginal and clitoral stimulation by leaning backwards, forwards or sitting upright. Leaning forward will increase clitoral stimulation, while leaning backwards will enhance vaginal stimulation – all while maintaining eye contact. Lying completely flat on her man will give her the greatest clitoral stimulation of all.

If a woman is feeling energetic (and it sure beats the gym to burn off those calories!) then she can squat on her feet and rock up and down over her partner's penis. This also enables her to tease a little, by letting her man's penis drift over her vagina before actual penetration.

Another variation is for a woman to turn the other way and face a man's feet rather than his head, known as the reverse cowgirl. Due to the natural upward angle of the penis, this can achieve direct G-spot stimulation too.

Woman on top – the ins

- A woman assumes the controls and is in the driving seat – sexy for both partners.
- Depth, speed and angle of penetration are all under the woman's control, making her feel less worried about whether her man's penis might thrust too deeply or cause her pain.
- A man gets a great view of what's going on – he can see a woman's body in detail, watch her face as she works her stuff and gets to see his penis going in and out of her vagina.
- The pressure is off the man to make an effort, except lie back and enjoy it – traditionally the woman's role.
- A man's hands are free (unless a woman has decided to restrain them in some way!) leaving him free to stroke and caress his partner's breasts, nipples and clitoris if she's in the upright position.

- A woman is hands-free enough to reach her own clitoris, giving her additional self-stimulation.
- A woman can turn her man on even more by fondling her own breasts, neck and shoulders.
- By pushing her shoulders back while sitting astride a man, her breasts 'magically' lift and her tummy sucks in!

Woman on top – the outs

- It can get tiring for a woman to be doing all the work!
- Some women are not confident about exposing so much of their body during sex.
- Some men find the passive role they have to take a little unnerving – if that's you, you need to get over yourself, fast!
- It can be difficult to maintain a regular rhythm for the woman, as she can get weary quickly, meaning that a man may not always achieve the perfect climax.
- If a man's penis is not fully erect, it can be difficult to establish penetrative sex and if you do manage it, it's easy to bend or twist the penis causing some discomfort or pain.

Rear-entry sex – doggy style

Doggy-style intercourse – named for pretty obvious reasons – is one of the most exciting sexual positions, because it allows seriously deep penetration. But more than that, there's something hot, sexy and primeval about having sex doggy style.

The position involves the woman kneeling, face down, on the bed – or on the floor, but beware of carpet burns – using the bed head or her hands and arms to give her support. The man kneels, or stands at the end of the bed, while he penetrates the woman's vagina.

A man can feel in control and dominant during rear-entry sex. He loves the urgency and animal aggression of doggy-style sex. His view is of a fabulous, sexy, yielding bottom in the air, tipped at just the right angle to ensure maximum vaginal penetration and just the hint of possibility of anal penetration too. The shape of a woman's body is incredibly erotic in this position too. While your bottom is in the air, there's a streamlined and curvy look to your body as it disappears into your waist, while your breasts are usually hanging fully below your body whatever your actual cup size. He can't see your face, so it's slightly anonymous too, like having sex with a stranger. He can also see his penis thrusting in and out of your vagina and his testicles might also get a surge of extra stimulation as they press against you. This is a truly heady mix of fantasy and intense physical pleasure for a man – no wonder guys love this position.

However it's not the best position for a man who is prone to climax too early, as all that powerful thrusting and visual and physical stimulation can make him come pretty speedily. It's perfect for a quickie or 'finishing off' though, especially if either partner has started to get tired from doing most of the work in other positions.

It's an incredibly submissive position for a woman, with little chance of controlling the speed or depth of penetration, so it's perfect for uninhibited women who enjoy the wilder side of sex. You can't see him, so you can let your imagination run riot and feel all that pleasure with little distraction. Because the penis is thrusting so deeply and pushing against the front wall of the vagina and the G-spot, this is a great way for you to have a vaginal orgasm too. The downside for you is that with little control over the depth of penetration, it can start to feel just too deep and full on at times, as the powerfully thrusting penis can hit the cervix, right at the back of the vagina with a bit of an 'ouch' moment!

However, you can adjust your position upwards slightly to avoid this – or ask your man to slow down a little or not lunge quite so deeply. If this feel like a good position for you and your partner, add a little extra spice to proceedings by doing it in front of a mirror where you can both watch what's going on.

Side by side: spooning

Side by side sex, or spooning, is lovely, languid, lazy sex. Lying like a pair of spoons, nestled into each other, in an almost foetal position, it's intimate and sensual rather than wild and acrobatic.

The man faces the back of the woman and enters her vagina from behind – so it is rear-entry sex, but without the deep penetration and animalistic rhythm. She draws her legs up towards her, with her bottom pushed towards her lover, to allow penetration. By bringing her knees up to her chest, she can alter the angle of entry and depth of penetration. It means that her partner can cuddle and hug her while having great sex at the same time.

It also helps if a guy tends to climax too easily, as it enables him to take his time, while still being able to stroke and caress his partner's breasts, neck and back. He can also reach round and use his fingers to arouse her clitoris, while she can reach back to play with his penis while he moves in and out of her body. The woman may need this extra clitoral stimulation to come to orgasm in this position, as penetration is fairly gentle and may not allow for the deep thrusting that vaginal orgasms usually need.

However, it's a very, relaxed, undemanding position and it also means that you can both fall asleep after sex, just as you are!

Some men spoon first thing in the morning, as they tend to wake up with an erection, and the temptation of a woman lying there, sleepy and gentle, can be very seductive. Some women love this – while others might find it a bit 'sneaky' – but it can be a little uncomfortable as the vagina isn't aroused or moist at this stage of course.

The quickie

Strictly speaking, having a quickie isn't really a sexual 'position' at all. It's urgent, exciting and can be adapted from all sorts of techniques. The quickie is hugely underrated. Although I spend much of my time explaining and writing about the finer detail of having sex, don't be fooled into thinking that the rip-your-clothes-off-now urgency of fast sex, isn't just as important in a relationship. As part of your sexual repertoire it can be every bit as fulfilling, sometimes more than, the longer and more intimate sex sessions.

Having a quickie is not about special foreplay techniques, doing it 'right' or ensuring that the ambience is special and the sheets clean. It is spontaneous, rushed and erotic. Drenched in lust and desire, you literally *have* to have sex, or you feel that you're about to burst. You can have a quickie on the stairs as you come in through the front door, on the sofa as soon as the mood strikes or on the bed semi-clothed. In any position that feels good to the both of you.

There is nothing not to like about quickie sex – it's a high-rolling adrenalin rush of deliciousness and a fast track to orgasm. It's the stuff of fantasies, yet available on a staircase, dining room table, or a car seat near you . . .

QUICKIE TRICKS

- Quickies aren't about removing your clothes carefully and folding them up neatly on the bedroom chair. A quickie is best done when your clothes are half off – trousers unzipped or panties pushed to one side.
- Any foreplay should be restricted to written or verbal only. Text your partner to tell them that you're in the mood and get them feeling the same way. Or call them and talk dirty to them when you're on your way home.

- Public, naughty quickies are fabulous. Your flatmate due back at any moment? A quiet part of the woods or beach on a sunny day? In a bar or restaurant when the mood takes you and the loos or a corridor are close by? All great, and ever-so-slightly-risky moments for the quickie.

- Quickies work best when both partners have the same urgent desires and can be as spontaneous as possible.

- It works well if one – or both of you – are tired, but you still want to have a little undemanding and brief fun.

- Kissing (sadly) is one of the first things to be neglected in a long-term relationship. There is nearly always urgent, frantic deep snogging during a quickie – enjoy!

- Quickies give you the chance to explore all sorts of different positions that you might not always bother with – it's an easy boost to a flagging sex life.

- It fires up the imagination rapidly. Feeling horny when you're driving? Pull over to a quiet lay-by (discreetly and under cover of darkness only!) and get down to it. Meal preparation getting dull? Lift her onto the kitchen work surface and work up a head of steam. Working late in the office and everyone else has gone home? The boardroom table beckons. It's as daring and as impulsive as you want it to be . . .

- Men find it very sexy when women initiate sex – a quickie is the perfect way to fire him up.

- Spice it up by wearing easy access clothes and underwear. No one wants to be fiddling with complicated fastenings during a quickie – it takes the heat out of the moment.

In spite of the deliciousness of these basic positions, there are way many more others, just waiting to be discovered. Read on . . .

5 More Positions: Expanding Your Repertoire

There are around a staggering 600 different positions – and more names for those positions – more than I could ever begin to describe in this chapter! However, the aim of this book is not to describe in detail every position ever created, but simply to suggest a few ideas of relatively simple sexual positions, that will encourage you to expand your repertoire and keep your sex life fresh, spontaneous and exciting, whether you enjoy a number of different sexual partners or are in a relationship for keeps.

We've already looked at the five basic positions, and a couple of variants on those, and you might well think that's enough to keep you going for a lifetime. And indeed it might be. Just as years ago we had fish on a Friday and spaghetti Bolognese was considered an exotic Italian dish. While we've moved on a bit in our eating habits, so we have in our sexual desires. We might love a regular Sunday roast (probably the equivalent of enjoyable, comfortable and familiar missionary position sex) and the occasional Big Mac and fries (the foodie version of a quickie – when you've gotta have it, you've gotta have it) but generally our eating habits have become more adventurous and we're increasingly willing to try something new in terms of taste, cuisine and where we eat out. It keeps our taste buds and our love of food alive, as well as being more special when we're in good company. And so it is with sex. Take it out of the bedroom, try it differently and savour something you've never tried before on a regular basis. Apart from the fact that you might find you love it (or hate it, so move on to something else new) it keeps your relationship fresh and you and your partner are a whole lot less likely to stray if you're getting a full and varied menu at home.

You probably won't want to try all of these positions – and some are pretty challenging for all but the most supple and bold of us – but I hope they'll give you food for thought at least and help you understand just how versatile the seemingly simple act of penetrative intercourse can be.

Coital Alignment Technique (CAT)

This slightly off-putting and scientific-sounding technique is actually a lot more fun than it sounds. CAT is a sexual position that seriously improves a woman's chances of achieving an orgasm through vaginal penetration. Developed by the American psychotherapist Edward Eichel, only a generation ago (so pretty brand spanking new in sexual position terms), it also increases the chances of simultaneous orgasm. Which, believe it or not, is quite a breakthrough.

Although simultaneous orgasm is deemed to be the nirvana of penetrative sex, it's actually pretty rare. If any of you guys out there think it's pretty commonplace that your partner comes at the same time as you, I hate to be the one to rain on your parade, but the chances are that she's faking it to please you . . .

Given that, at a conservative estimate, two thirds of women need clitoral, rather than vaginal stimulation, to come to orgasm, Eichel realised that the classic missionary position was fairly useless at bringing a woman to climax, as the in and out thrusting motion missed the clitoris itself by quite a few centimetres. So he 'developed' a rocking and rolling motion, that keeps pressure on the clitoris during vaginal intercourse, making it much easier for a woman to achieve orgasm this way. By allowing a combined thrusting from both partners – rather than simply having the man do all the work – and having sex at a higher angle than usual – the woman hugely increases her chances of having an orgasm during penetrative sex.

How to do it

OK, so given that CAT is probably the best technique for the all-important clitoral stimulation during sex, it's actually not all that easy and takes a bit of practice and commitment, especially as it involves 'undoing' most of what has become second nature, sexually speaking, over the years.

CAT is essentially a variation on the classic missionary position, with the guy on top, face to face with his partner. Getting into the standard missionary position, a man has to use his penis to just begin to penetrate his partner in the usual way, and then lift himself further up the length of her body, so that his thrusting penis is making contact with her clitoris. Both partners' pelvises should be level at this stage. He needs to relax his upper body, while pressing his weight onto her, with his arms cupping her shoulders, by coming up and over her armpits with the flat of his hands, rather than propping himself up on his elbows. This makes him slide forwards and higher, towards the woman's shoulders and head. She needs to shimmy up a few centimetres, once her partner's penis is fully inside her, so that she can grind her clitoris against his pubic bone. She should then wrap her legs around his thighs, extending the stretch of her legs, so that her ankles are resting on his calves. In this position she can thrust her own pelvis, which makes constant contact between her clitoris and the base of his penis. She will lead on the upward movement, pushing upwards with her pelvis, when penetration will be at its deepest. The man pushes more during the downward movement, increasing clitoral pressure from the base of his penis. Penetration is shallower on the downward thrust.

By moving your pelvis in this way, the to and fro rocking movement changes the emphasis from internal vaginal stimulation to external clitoral stimulation. It's important to keep this motion going on a rhythmical and consistent level, which is identical for both of you. Coordination is essential here and it can be difficult for a man to get used to resisting his own urge to thrust. As I said, this can take some practice and undoing of long-held habits. But it should start to feel like pressure and counter-pressure, rather than in and out thrusting, on the upward and downwards strokes. And unlike traditional thrusting, which tends to speed up towards climax, you need to keep a steady, even pace going throughout. Don't be put off by the lengthy and slightly technical explanation of the ins and outs of CAT – once you've got used to it, it can be hugely pleasurable as far as your orgasms are concerned and you'll soon find that you can both climax together, which has got to be the best way in the world to provide the denouement to any sex session.

CAT can be done in the standard missionary position, or with the woman on top, lying over her lover, with her legs inside his.

Chair sex

There's a lot of fun to be had from using a chair, sofa or recliner as a prop during sex. It allows easy repositioning, balance and enhances control during dominance games, as the 'sitter' has little natural mobility while the 'straddler' does most of the work!

Milk and water embrace

The milk and water embrace is a well-known position from the *Kama Sutra* and it's the woman taking control here. The man sits on an upright but comfortable chair, while the woman sits astride his lap, facing away from him. The man wraps the woman in his arms, then she can guide his fingers to play with her labia and clitoris. And while this feast of pleasure is going on, she can clench the cheeks of her bottom around his penis, squeezing and stimulating it, feeling him grow harder under her movements.

Once she is aroused and ready for penetration, she needs to lift herself up slightly and lower herself down onto his hard penis. Once he is inside the woman – and penetration during the milk and water embrace can be very deep – she can rock back and forth, while lowering herself up and down to achieve extra thrusts.

Although this is fabulous for feeling in control, as well as giving a great work out to the woman's inner thighs, it can get a little tiring after a while as, all that raising and lowering to maximise depth of penetration can make your legs ache!

Lean back and enjoy

The man should sit back on a comfortable, slouchy chair while the woman sits facing him, straddling his lap with her legs splayed apart and her knees drawn up towards his chest. Once he has fully penetrated his partner, she should use his penis as an 'anchor' to allow herself to gently lean back so that she's almost upside down with her arms outstretched behind her to the floor.

This position gives the man a seriously naughty view of the woman's vagina in all its outstretched glory, and provided she can balance on her arms (and squeeze her vaginal muscles at the same time) she can take control of the speed, timing and intensity of thrusts to suit both partners.

Take this one slowly, as not only does the blood rush to the woman's head if done too fast it can cause the man's penis to bend at an awkward and painful angle or slip out altogether. This position is not for the faint-hearted, but like so many of these more athletic positions, a little practice can make perfect . . .

Lounging about

This is essentially the woman on top position described on page 105, but it is fabulous for outdoor sex, as it's best done on a reclining sun lounger or narrow bench. He should lie down, face up, with his arms at his side and his legs together. Facing his feet, the woman sits astride him, straddling his lap and planting both of her feet firmly on the ground.

Then she should literally back herself down towards his penis, rocking backwards and forwards over the head of his penis to bring him to full arousal. When he feels just right, the woman should move herself down over him to let him enter her. Then she should move backwards and forwards, up and down and side to side.

Not only will he love watching her bottom strutting its stuff as it moves around up and over his penis, she can control the circular motions to ensure that she has the most amazing sensations on the back wall of her vagina. As she rides him, she should use one hand to hold him for support and the other to stroke his perineum, testicles and her own clitoris.

Pounding the spot

Pounding the spot is a slightly more athletic position, which can lead on from the milk and water embrace. While clasping her hands tightly around her man's neck, she can literally throw back her head and arch her spine, allowing all her weight to be supported on her clasped hands and arms.

By raising her feet a little and sliding her bottom into place, he can grip her hips and manoeuvre his penis, so that he can pull her up and down on him, in a rhythmical, pulsating motion. By raising and lowering her legs, she can lever herself so that she can get clitoral stimulation as well as vaginal stimulation – literally pounding the spot. This position produces deep, intense and fast thrusts that can be controlled by either partner – useful, as it can be quite tiring after a while on her legs and arms.

The lotus position

The lotus position is a traditional sitting yoga position. It's classic stuff and while it needs a little dexterity and practice, as it's not always easy to get penetration spot on the first time, it's a really intimate and sensual technique. The partners sit opposite each other and make direct eye contact. Both partners have complete views of each other's faces and bodies, which adds to the build-up of excitement. It also allows you to kiss, nuzzle and touch each other's bodies while maintaining eye contact – and is an especially erotic position if performed while bathed in gentle candle light.

The man sits with his legs crossed at the ankle and uses his hand to make his penis as erect as possible. Sitting opposite, propped up on a couple of cushions if she needs to – it also helps prevent bending his penis during penetration – the woman then moves towards her lover and sits astride him, wrapping her legs and arms around his back. Rather than using a thrusting up and down motion, she needs to clench and unclench her vaginal muscles, maintaining just enough movement to keep the man hard and excited, but not so much that he is tempted to orgasm too quickly. Maintaining this position, the partners can gently rock together and towards each other, which also allows stimulation of the woman's G-spot. Although the lotus position doesn't involve vigorous thrusting, it is possible to achieve deep penetration.

Splitting the bamboo

Another graphically and suggestively named position from the *Kama Sutra*, splitting the bamboo is an erotic and not-too-difficult-to-achieve technique that can really enhance and add another dimension to your sex life.

Lying down on the bed, the woman rests her ankles on her man's shoulders while he kneels, legs apart, around her bottom. This can be quite a sensitive position for the woman, as her vagina is shortened, so the man needs to enter slowly and carefully. Once he is inside her, she can place one foot on his chest, while the other remains on his shoulder.

It's important that the man stays quite still and resists thrusting or moving, as it is simply the position of her legs and back that dictate pace and rhythm. As she moves her legs into slightly different angles, her vagina will squeeze and tighten against his penis, giving you both a lazy, but delicious pulsating sensation that can bring you both to an intense orgasm, whenever you're ready.

Pressing

Not dissimilar to splitting the bamboo, the pressing position is a faster, deeper and more intense version.

While lying down the woman should raise both of her legs and place the soles of her feet flat on the man's chest while keeping her thighs tightly squeezed together. He should hold onto her feet to keep her steady. As the man penetrates her, it will feel deep and sharp, but incredibly intense. If she feels any pain, pushing her feet harder against his chest will give him the message to pull away a little. It's a highly erotic position for both partners, and the man especially enjoys this as he can see his penis sliding in and out of her vagina with each thrust. This position, as with so many based on *Kama Sutra* techniques, both shortens and tightens the vagina, making for a tight and exciting fit!

While he is in control of the rhythm, she can move her hips from side to side to vary the pace and if the man holds her knees together, she can intensify the grip on his penis and this can feel sensational for both partners.

Camel's hump

The camel's hump is like a standing doggy position, which produces deep and intense thrusting. The woman stands up, with her feet slightly apart, resting her elbows and lower arms on a sofa or bed, linen basket or chair back, using a few cushions or pillows if necessary s to get comfortable.

The man stands behind her and gets an amazingly erotic

and clear view of the woman's labia, spread open before him – virtually guaranteed to make him erect pretty swiftly. He can then use the tip of his penis to gently tease his partner's labia, push himself gently into her vagina and then pull away again, arousing her further with each tantalising push. Rather than thrust away in an urgent fashion, tempted though he might be, the man should build up with shorter, briefer thrusts before entering the woman fully.

Off the wall

This is the stuff of fantasy, with the man displaying a macho show of strength and power at the same time. While the woman leans with her back against a wall, he should stand in front of her. As he bends a little, she wraps her arms tightly around his neck, and pulls herself up around him, with her legs wrapped around him.

The woman should keep her back and head against the wall, to keep her balance, and as he penetrates her, cupping her thighs and bottom for support, she should let her legs drop down a little, while still keeping her feet curled in around the back of his thighs.

This is a great position for the man to maintain an erection, as the blood is needed throughout his body to give him strength and his erection is not so intense.

The starfish

Both partners should lie on the bed, backs down and face up, but lying across each other in opposite directions, so that the woman is on top, nestling the back of her head between her lover's legs. They then manoeuvre into a scissor-like position and she allows her lover to penetrate her, while both partners can use their hands to grip onto the other's legs for support and balance.

This position is great for the angle, pressure and grinding movement against the woman's clitoris and so increases her chances of orgasm. It works in harmony and unison, so that if both partners arch their backs, for instance, you can achieve a deeper penetration.

The butterfly

The man needs to kneel with his legs bent underneath him as she climbs onto his lap and slides over his erect penis, allowing him to penetrate her fully in one assured movement. While embracing him, she should start to gently bounce up and down on his penis, squeezing her pelvic floor muscles in a regular rhythm, imitating the fluttering wings of a butterfly in flight.

He then lifts himself up, taking his weight on his knees, with one foot flat on the bed for support and balance. She should stretch out her legs, into an outstretched butterfly wing position, while leaning back to intensify the pressure. As the man will be taking most of the woman's weight, it's unlikely that he'll be able to pound away with major thrusts, but the angle and intimacy of this position have their own special rewards.

Doing this slowly and with perfect balance and harmony, you'll soon feel like you're flying!

The twining position

This is one of the first positions named in the *Kama Sutra* and is one of the easiest positions to achieve – giving an intimate, full body contact pose – as well as being quick to build up arousal.

Both partners lie on their sides, facing one another, and while they look deep into each other's eyes, they let their limbs entwine. She can then let her legs part slightly, allowing the man to penetrate her vaginally. By straddling her upper thigh across her lover, she can pull him in towards her and raise or lower her leg to adjust speed, intensity and depth. Even though it's a simple enough twist on the standard missionary position, it does allow her to take control over his thrusting and encourages him to do a little more circling and grinding than straightforward pumping and thrusting.

Once both partners are stimulated and aroused, the man can raise himself up onto his knees, while the woman remains in the lying position.

The pick me up

The pick me up also involves entwining limbs, so it's similar to the twining position but with a little more dexterity and strength needed on the man's part.

The pick me up begins with the woman sitting opposite her partner on the edge of the bed. The man squats down, taking his weight on his bended legs. The woman takes his penis in her hands, giving him a twist and turn hand job to bring him to a full erection. She then guides herself down over his penis to achieve penetration. Once he is deep inside her, she wraps her legs tightly around his middle and crosses her legs, with her feet in a locked position, around his bottom.

While she draws her arms around his shoulders for support, the man slowly brings himself to a standing position. He will need to rise up very slowly, giving the woman support under her thighs and bottom and keeping her close to his body, his legs becoming rigid whilst he swings her into him in short, swift thrusts.

This can be a very erotic and powerful position and the tensile strength needed by the man can bring him to an orgasm quite quickly. In order for a woman to climax, she must feel safe and secure in his grasp, so this position is not for the faint-hearted.

The see-saw

The see-saw can feel very sexy and self-indulgent, as it allows the woman to feel both supported and wild. While the man is lying down, she should sit on top of him, pressing her legs tightly against his sides and tucking her feet under his thighs for support. She then slips slowly down onto his erect penis, allowing her hands to slip down his arms, until both partners are clutching each other firmly by the wrists. While you're both interlocked in a rhythmical swinging backwards and forwards motion, you can go as far back as you like, while it still feels good.

Neither partner assumes control in this position and it requires intimacy, trust and support. She should be careful not to pull back too far though, as it's easy for her partner's penis to slip out of her during the see-saw, somewhat dampening the mood! It can also pull hard on her back and arms, so a few strategically placed cushions for support can help.

Figure of eight

The woman should lie on the floor, face up, with a couple of cushions or pillows supporting her bottom. With wide-open legs and slightly bent knees, she should keep her arms high above her head so that she is completely flexed open. The man should then penetrate the woman at a fairly high angle, pushing his hands on the floor beside her head for support. He should then move inside her with slow, deliberate figure of eight motions so that she can feel his penis tracing the number inside her like a coiled snake.

In this position his pubic bone will rub against her clitoris, so she'll feel sensual and deeply aroused at the same time. Like many of these positions, this should be done with a slow, steady build-up, increasing the woman's chances of a highly powerful and fulfilling climax. The high angle of penetration also increases the chance of hitting the G-spot.

Bottoms up

Remember those roly-poly exercises you did when you were a kid? Where you lay flat on your back and pushed your legs behind you and over your head as far as they would go without collapsing into fits of giggles? Good – because this is just the supple position you need to adopt for bottoms up. Only without the falling over and maybe without the giggles too . . .

Once the woman has leaned back, with her back arched and legs as far back as they'll go, he should be down on his bended knees leaning forward, facing directly over her, using the palms of his hand for support on the floor (beds are a bit too bouncy and yielding for this one!) as he enters her. This position narrows and contracts the woman's vagina, allowing for a really tight fit and deep penetration. Thrusting will cause both partners to lose balance, so you'll both need to rock too and fro, and she can alter the access and depth of penetration by widening and closing her legs.

Let us pray

Although the man doesn't actually have his hands together in the praying position, he is kneeling down sitting on his legs, with his back in an erect and rather respectful posture. His head is also bowed gracefully as he watches the woman's vagina intently. She lies down on her back, with her bottom nestled in his crotch, her legs up, knees bent and feet crossed over his chest.

While her hands are free to caress his thighs, his hands are firmly in the driving seat, as he uses them to manoeuvre her bottom and upper thighs around to take that longing look at her open vagina and allow him to slide in.

The man can also raise himself onto his knees, pulling his lover higher with him. She remains in the same position, only higher, forming an inverted 'S' shape as her back is arched further off the floor or bed.

This position can be done on the bed, the carpet or even outdoors on the grass or on the beach. It is slow, sensuous and very erotic as you can simply close your eyes, lie back and enjoy.

Riding the horse

Riding the horse is not the conventional position that you might expect from its name. The man should lie down on the bed, face up, while she kneels between his open legs. She gets a wonderful view of his genitals and can use this moment to stroke, brush and tease his inner thighs and whole genital area with soft, delicate movements. The man will love this and the woman can watch the pleasure on his face and sense his breathing quicken as she takes control and masturbates him slowly. When the man feels aroused and almost fully erect, he should pull his knees up towards his chest, while she also kneels up and presses herself down so that each partner's genitals are just touching each other.

She then uses his thighs to lean further forwards, while his feet lock over her shoulders, and lower herself down fully onto his penis, controlling the soft and slow thrusts at her own pace.

Outdoors sex

Having sex outdoors is becoming something of a forgotten pleasure. In previous generations, when we lived with our parents for longer and when pre-marital sex was still an issue, outdoors sex was much more common. Whether it was in the car in a secluded car park, in a field on a sunny day or on the beach, behind a handy sand dune or two – having sex in the great outdoors was more commonplace, and was borne out of necessity. Where else were you going to go for your illicit pleasures?

These days we have our own homes, families are more accepting, we travel more and can book a hotel room for the night without having to pretend to be Mr and Mrs Smith. This means that outdoor sex is no longer the only option on offer. But outdoors sex has always been naughty, daring and imbued with the danger of being caught out. Which for some is a huge turn-on – pounding hearts, fresh air and the adrenalin rush of being caught out simply adds to the excitement.

OK, yes I know it's illegal to have sex in public. I also know that it can carry a jail sentence if you're caught and reported. So you've got to be sensible about it – take simple precautions like covering yourselves with a picnic blanket or beach umbrella. And best done in a less crowded place, well away from families enjoying a picnic or a day on the beach. While sex in public is illegal and I don't condone the breaking of the law, if you're clever and discreet, you can indulge yourselves in the thrill and pleasure rush that al fresco sex offers up.

In the car

Sex in the back seat of a car in a dark secluded car park used to be a bit of steamy-windowed fun. Sadly these days it's got itself a bit of a sleazy reputation, thanks to the reports of a few high-profile celebs, who have been caught 'dogging' in car parks. Not to be confused with 'doggy style', dogging is the practice of having sex in a semi-public place with a view to being watched, rather than in seclusion and privacy, or simply going along to watch others.

Car parks, frequented by the dogging fraternity, are often well known, so if you're going for a little back-seat action, these car parks are best avoided. Try a quiet street or country lane instead. Sex in a car can be fun – you can't do it missionary style (unless you've got some fancy rear-seat-folding-flat affair in your car) so you have to get into all sorts of athletic and unlikely positions to avoid gear stick, door handle or seat belt-related injuries! So it's definitely a challenge . . .

However, it's much sexier to have sex on the car bonnet. Sure, it's much more risky too, being that much more exposed, but that just adds to the thrill. It's sensible to choose a secluded country lane or similar. Make sure that the car engine is cool – if you've been driving around for a while, it can be bottom-searingly hot. And if you're doing it from cold, make sure you put a coat or a blanket over the top, when the reverse can be true on a chilly day!

The bonnet is the perfect height for the woman to jump up and lie or sit down on it, with her legs open, while her man stands in front of her. She can pull him into penetrative sex by wrapping her legs tightly around his middle.

On the beach

The thing that makes sex in the sand so erotic and exciting is in part due to the fact that beachside holidays are already imbued with a massive sense of romanticism and escapism, so just the thought of sex in the sand can make your toes tingle. Plus most people are already semi-naked, enjoying the comforting warmth of the sun and taking pleasure in those long, languid, lazy days.

Massaging sun lotion into each other is a fabulous way to kick start sex in the sand, and you can sculpt soft sand into the kind of dip and shape that makes it most comfortable to have sex. And sex on the beach after a few hours' lazing in the sun means that the deliciousness is all the more intense as your sun-warmed bodies entwine with each other. Of course one of the downsides to sex on the beach is gritty, coarse sand ending up deep in the crevices of some especially sensitive places, so the finer the sand the better. You can use a blanket or a towel of course, or even a sun lounger, but if you do find sand creeping into some of your genital folds, simply enjoy the pleasure of each other and showering it off together, once you get back home to your home or hotel. And you thought Sex on the Beach was just a sickly tasting cocktail . . .

In the sea

The sea – or secluded pool – is a fabulous place to enjoy sex. The water disguises anything going on below neck or waist level and we all feel supple and agile in the water, due to the feeling of weightlessness and buoyancy.

You can have sex deep out to sea – after diving from a boat – in the shallow end of a pool or recreate that wonderfully romantic scene from the Hollywood movie *From Here to Eternity* where you're rolling about in the sandy shallows of the lapping waves, on the shore, feeling the sea on your naked bodies as it pulls back and forth.

In the garden

If you're lucky, you'll have a nice secluded garden with mature shrubs, a lawn and patio area and little chance of curious neighbours overlooking your al fresco activities. If not, then try it after dark or consider that maybe the thought of being seen might just add to the frisson of it all.

Most people love the earthy, clean smell of freshly mown grass with its connotations of summer days of promise and expectation. So what better place to throw down a picnic blanket and make love. The fresh air makes us feel energised and happy and we associate playing in the garden with being a child and the freedom that went with that period of our lives.

You can do anything on the grass that you could do on the carpet and most things that you can do on a bed, so let your imagination – and some of the positions listed in this chapter – take over.

Or use your patio or picnic table as a prop. Place a rug or duvet down on the table, lie or sit down, wrap your legs around your man as he stands in front of you and enjoy.

On a boat

Of course a boat could mean anything from a small fishing or rowing boat up to a multi-storey cruise liner. One thing they all have in common is that seductive, relaxing bobbing motion of the sea – unless of course you're in a Force 10 gale, in which case the experience could be somewhat different!

Generally boats are sexy, romantic places with a soft breeze on deck and if you're doing it at night, there might be a vast star-studded sky to look up on too. There are all those handy props around as well. Safety rails to hang on to and padded deck loungers to take any potential discomfort away. What could be lovelier than having sex on a boat?

On the hotel balcony

Whether you're staying at the smartest of upmarket hotels or a simple country apartment, a balcony usually gives you fabulous views of the surrounding area as well as being secluded enough to not be too high risk at getting caught out.

Take out a bottle of champagne, something sexy to eat like strawberries, chocolate, figs or olives and indulge your-selves as the sun sets. Then either put the duvet or a thick blanket down on the balcony floor – they're usually made of pretty stern stuff like marble or concrete, so protect your sensitive parts – and snuggle under the stars to be as naughty and as daring as the mood takes you.

Up against a tree

A smooth-barked tree, especially in full foliage with dappled, sheltered sunlight filtering through is a beautiful place to get back to basics, as nature intended.

You need to stand leaning back against the tree, with your lover in front of you. Clasp your hands around his neck and jump on board, wrapping your legs tightly around his middle. This is an outdoors version of the pick me up and is perfect for a sneaky quickie.

For all this talk about the myriad and exotic positions we can adopt to enhance our sex lives, none of it is likely to offer us enough excitement and ultimate fulfilment unless we can actually reach a climax. And so the next chapter is solely devoted to the intimate knowledge and sublime pleasure of the orgasm.

6 Orgasm: Hers, His, Making it the Best

Orgasm. The Big 'O'. This is the big one – the very purpose of having sex for pleasure rather than reproduction. If sex is travelling, then having an orgasm is arriving to a luxurious, exotic destination with not a care in the world.

So why can it be so elusive? Not for men generally – the very thought of a random woman, in all her naked glory, can set his climax off. But for us women it can be complicated, rare and difficult to achieve, at least with any regularity.

Mother Nature can be a capricious creature. Why did she tuck away, in a reasonably hard-to-find place, our clitoris – this tiny little flap of skin, our mini-penis, which is meant to be the key to ultimate pleasure? She left it clearly hanging on the outside for guys, so why hide ours? Maybe it's a simple design fault. Or maybe we just have to work a little harder at finding the right sort of positions to satisfy our cravings. And get our men to work a little harder with their penises, tongues, mouths and hands to make sure we're pleased. So maybe it's not a design fault, merely a clever piece of natural trickery to ensure that we have to have a little variety in our sex lives to ensure pleasure rather than simply procreation.

The female orgasm has certainly provided plenty of provocative research and debate over the last couple of thousand years. Controversy continues to rage over how many different types of female orgasm exist. There's clitoral orgasm, vaginal orgasm and blended orgasm (basically a mixture of clitoral and vaginal orgasm) for starters. Whatever you read about the types of orgasm, the truth is that physiologically, it's all pretty much the same thing – both for men and women. At its simplest, it is the body releasing blood back into the bloodstream after it has been aroused, causing involuntary muscle contractions followed by a sudden release of euphoria. The word orgasm comes from the Greek *orgainein*, meaning to swell, as in swelling with lust. But while the physiological mechanics might be the same each time, the emotional interpretation – our feelings – won't always be the same. We can have gentle, delicate and pleasing orgasms or we can have toe-curling, head-dizzying frenzied orgasms that can feel quite otherworldly. Whether your legs turn to jelly or you simply feel a pleasant glow will depend on many factors including how relaxed you are, how aroused you feel and the sensitivity and intimacy of your partner.

My view is that for the vast majority of women, well over two-thirds, there has to be some direct stimulation of the clitoris to achieve an orgasm. The other 'lucky' third can achieve orgasm through vaginal penetration alone. Because the clitoris is such an important part of our sexual goody bag, and jam-packed with far more nerve endings than our vagina, I suspect that these women actually *don't* climax through vaginal penetration only. I suspect that they either have a larger-than-average clitoris or have a clitoris that is closer than usual to the vaginal opening. Or it could be that their lover is using a circular, grinding motion when he is thrusting in and out of them, thus causing stimulation against the clitoris, without the woman necessarily being aware of what is going on.

Whatever my views, or those of any other sexpert, what is not in doubt is that the clitoris is the epicentre of orgasmic pleasure and for any woman who wants to experience an orgasm at its finest (or even for the first time) this is a part of your body that you need to get to know intimately. And indeed, ensure that your lover is fully aware and comfortable with this little baby too.

Although your body is able to produce enough natural lubrication to enable you to have a great orgasm, the production of lubrication can vary enormously. It's highly dependent on a number of external factors including your stress levels, your time of the month, your mood and any medicines – either over the counter or prescription – that you might be taking at the time. So using a good water-based lubricant is pretty essential to having the best orgasm. Whether you are hoping to orgasm through penetrative sex or manually (your fingers or his!) lubricant allows the whole process to be more slippery and lets your hands glide at the right pressure and rhythm to give yourself the optimum chance of reaching your peak as effectively as possible.

The sexual response cycle

Climaxing, coming or having an orgasm is just one part of the sexual response cycle and it helps to know just what this is – although don't beat yourself up if you don't travel through these four distinct phases in order each and every time you have sex. We're all individuals and these phases vary according to our mood, situation and type of sex we're having. The sexual response cycle often works as it 'should' during long, languid sex but a quickie will understandably speed up or 'over-ride' these four phases.

The Human Sexual Response Cycle was identified by two American research pioneers, in the 1950s and 1960s, William H. Masters and Virginia E. Johnson. Masters and Johnson clearly identified four distinct phases of what happens to our bodies during sex.

The excitement phase

During the excitement phase, our breathing quickens, our nipples harden and our skin becomes flushed. Blood flows into the penis, engorging it and making it swell into an erection, while the testicles flatten and rise slightly. A small drop of clear, pre-ejaculate fluid also comes from the head of the penis. Meanwhile the walls of the vagina contract, producing a moist secretion and blood flows to the clitoris, making it swell and get darker and harder.

The plateau phase

Following on from the excitement phase, the plateau sees our blood pressure and our heart rate quicken even more and the penis becomes fully erect to the point where a man feels likely to climax at any moment. This is a stage of high arousal. Meanwhile the contractions of the vagina become stronger and faster, we release more lubrication and our labia and vaginal entrance darken even further.

The orgasmic phase

Your muscles tense even further and there is a feeling of intense pressure, physiologically, caused by the blood flow having redirected itself so much towards the genitals. This pressure cooker effect, builds up to a point where it has to be released, allowing the blood to flow normally throughout the rest of the body again. This release of blood and the instant relaxation of the muscles is a fairly unsexy way of describing the orgasm itself! During the peak of pressure the semen is drawn up through the penis towards the head and a climax is inevitable. The penis contracts in spasm and the semen spurts out. Meanwhile, as the woman climaxes her vaginal lubrication increases even more and the vaginal walls start to contract spasmodically.

The resolution phase

As the blood flow starts to return to normal, your heart rate and blood pressure decreases. The penis shrinks back down to its flaccid state and the replenishment of energy and semen production begins once again. The vagina will lighten in colour and the clitoris will feel ultra-sensitive, due to the fact that this tiny 'sac' has been so engorged with blood and then it's all flowed away again in a moment.

How to have an orgasm

I don't imagine that there are many men reading this section who will want to know how to have an orgasm or wonder whether they have ever had one. The male orgasmic experience has its own problems but learning how to have one or not knowing whether you've had one, isn't one of them.

Women, however, often do wonder if they've ever experienced an orgasm. If this is you, and you've had a lovely but slightly vague feeling of sudden pleasure during sex, then you've probably had a much more gentle vaginal orgasm. Clitoral orgasms let you know they're around. The powerful, euphoric intensity of a clitoral orgasm is unmistakeable and leaves you in no doubt that something pretty amazing has just occurred. But you're most certainly not alone if you have never experienced an orgasm. Some women simply don't notice their orgasms, so gentle and tiny are their contractions, that they are not aware of having had an orgasm at all. However for most women, their lack of achieving an orgasm is usually down to guilt, due to a religious, strict or repressed upbringing for example. Or it could be the result of a simple lack of understanding of how their bodies work and what's what 'down below' in that complex part of our genitals, where so much is tucked way out of sight.

The first thing to do is to get to know, understand and appreciate your genitals. Opening your legs and taking a look at yourself while using a mirror is a good start. And learning how to masturbate and give yourself self-pleasure is another. See chapter 2, page 39 for more information on learning how to masturbate effectively.

If you've never managed to achieve an orgasm, these are my top five recommendations for best learning how to have one.

1 Firstly, it is often reassuring to understand that having an orgasm is learned behaviour not a natural, pre-programmed response or knee-jerk reflex. It won't suddenly happen to you while sitting on a train to work – although it *could* happen to you if you're thinking sexy, erotic thoughts and you feel a tingling between your legs.

2 Get to know, understand and appreciate your body – and that includes your breasts, your tummy, your thighs and not just your genitalia. Get to enjoy your own touch on your own body. Turn the lights down, the phone off and play some soft music and experiment with what feels good – from you to you.

3 Take this process further and learn how to masturbate effectively. Most women experience their first orgasm on their own – not with a partner. There are books like this one to help you learn to masturbate and toys like vibrators and dildos on every high street that will help you in the process. And use your hands – as every man knows, this is the best 'toy' possible for giving yourself a climax. You can also buy 'personal massagers' along with your shampoo and cotton wool buds in Boots these days, if you feel embarrassed going into a sex shop or buying online. These

are perfect for massaging your clitoris – the key to achieving your first orgasm.

4 Learn to love your vagina. It's self-cleaning, beautiful and your own personal route to intense pleasure. It's not dirty, you're not a bad person for getting to know and love it and there is nothing to feel guilty about in giving yourself some manual stimulation. Make time in your weekly – or even daily routine – to get to know yourself as intimately as possible. Remind yourself that you deserve this, even if only to communicate effectively with your partner about what feels good for you. Or learn how to be satisfied when you're between partners.

5 And learn to love your body. It's only by understanding how fabulous you are that you'll manage to relax enough to let go and actually manage an orgasm – it's key. Stress and anxiety are the single most serious inhibitors of achieving an orgasm. Most men are excited by the sight of a naked woman – whatever shape or size you are. But if you have concerns about the way you look then take a little time out to make improvements. Join the gym or slimming class or get a new haircut or a set of sexy lingerie that enhances your curves.

Most women lose the ability to orgasm at some point in their lives. If you are stressed, tired, anxious or have recently had a baby then it will be more difficult to achieve an orgasm, because your natural energy is dealing with other concerns. Some women find sex perfectly pleasurable without an orgasm and it's rarer than you might think to achieve one every time. But if you're in a long-term relationship and are regularly missing out on an orgasm or can't remember the last time the earth moved for you, then that's something to discuss with your partner. It's easy to get lazy sexually and men don't always pay you the same attention or make the same effort during sex that they might have done when your relationship was new and shiny or when he was trying to impress you sexually during the early stages. It's vitally important to keep the lines of communication over these sorts of issues open as they start to happen and before they become bigger issues with the resentment and damage, relationship wise, that can go with a dwindling sex life.

If you're no longer having orgasms and feel that you can't communicate this to your partner or simply don't feel inclined to – or have even begun to tense up during what has become the 'duty' of sex, then this is much more indicative of the fact that you may have a more serious problem in the relationship itself. Seeing sex as something that you have to do, as infrequently as possible, or making excuses not to find the time, rather than something you want to do and make special time for, may mean that this particular relationship is reaching its natural conclusion.

Faking it

There's a lot of controversy over faking an orgasm. The fact is that most women *have* faked an orgasm at some time or other: a recent and anonymous survey reported that a staggering 80% of women regularly fake orgasm during intercourse.

However, most are reluctant to admit to their closest gal-pals or partner that they are doing so, as it somehow implies that we've 'failed' to have a real one. So what are the real reasons why women fake an orgasm?

- We're too tired or too busy to take the requisite amount of time to indulge in foreplay and sex in order to achieve a genuine orgasm.
- Because we know how to do it (we've all seen *When Harry Met Sally*), how to do it well and men rarely notice that we're faking it.
- We don't want to upset our lover by implying that he wasn't good enough in bed to make us come. Or in spite of all that effort during oral sex, it was never likely to happen.
- Because we want to 'get it over and done with'. If your relationship is going through a rough patch or you're at the tail end of a relationship and your libido is diminishing as a result, you might just want to rush through your sexual 'duty' and get it over with as quickly as possible.
- If you find yourself fretting about your day at work tomorrow or whether your child is going to wake up in the middle of the night and you're simply not in a yielding mood, it's easier to fake an orgasm than to cause potential offence by telling him your mind was on much more mundane matters than your own pleasure.
- Fabulous, toe-curling, peel-yourself-off-the-ceiling clitoral orgasms don't happen every time (unlike the movies) and our fear of 'failure' makes it easier to fake than to make.

It might surprise you to know that men also fake orgasms. I know you think you'd be able to tell from the level of moisture after sex, but if he has produced pre-ejaculate and you have become lubricated, or you have been using lubrication, it's not as obvious as you'd think. Men also become tired or stressed, meaning that they can't always sustain an erection and it's easier to fake an orgasm than to admit that they've drooped halfway through vaginal intercourse.

Men also fake orgasms out of consideration to us. If they've worked magnificently hard at devoting themselves to making sure that you have a mind-blowing orgasm, then sometimes it's just easier to imply that they've had one too, rather than press his still erect penis onto your ultra-sensitive post orgasmic clitoris and vagina, just in case he hurts you.

My view is that if you're having 'proper' orgasms the vast majority of the time, you shouldn't beat yourself up over faking the occasional orgasm, if feeling stressed or tired, in order to please your partner.

Nine levels of orgasm

According to Taoist sexual practice, there are nine separate but overlapping stages to the female orgasm. Each level corresponds to an organ system and has observable signs. In most cases these levels tend to flow and intermingle, and it is the man's job to recognise when one level is complete and the next level has been entered, until all are completed. Which basically means that the man has to hold off his own orgasm until he has fulfilled his woman. While that sounds like perfect sex (for the woman at least!) it is good practice for a man to hold off his own orgasm, see page 165. In reality, most of us only reach stage of four of these nine phases, but it could certainly add a little Eastern excitement to your love-making to try them out. It's at stage five when things start to become more interesting, as you'll see, even though to our Western practices they seem rather bizarre. And these levels are supposed to have traditional health-giving and healing properties too. So it's a win-win situation all round!

These levels are:

Level 1: The lung organ system
The woman sighs, breathes heavily and salivates.

Level 2: The heart
The woman, while kissing the man, extends her tongue to him. The tip of the tongue, according to Taoist theory corresponds to the heart, so she is in effect reaching out to him with her heart.

Level 3: Spleen, pancreas and stomach
As her muscles become activated, the woman grasps and holds the man tightly as if taking him in as one takes in food.

Level 4: Kidneys and bladder
The woman experiences a series of vaginal spasms and secretions begin to flow. It is at this point that most of us believe

that the woman has had her orgasm. Like the man, she begins to relax as her joints loosen.

Level 5: Bones

Her bones loosen and joints loosen and she begins to bite the man.

Level 6: Liver and nerves

The woman undulates and gyrates like a snake, trying to wrap her arms and legs around the man.

Level 7: Blood

Her blood begins to 'boil' and she is frantically trying to touch the man everywhere.

Level 8: Muscles

Her muscles totally relax. She bites even more and grabs the man's nipples.

Level 9: The entire body is energised

She totally collapses in a 'little death'. She has completely surrendered to her man.

G-spot

If the clitoris is the magic trigger for most women, the G-spot is a hell of a close runner-up. The G-spot – or to give it its full name of the Grafenberg spot – is a wonderful, special, highly sensitive area that you and your partner need to find and experiment with at your earliest opportunity. The elusive G-spot has been the subject of much speculation and the butt of many dinner party and locker room jokes. Does it exist? Where is it? Do we all have one? And if your man can find yours, and work it effectively, you'll probably want to marry him. We women owe a huge debt of gratitude to the German gynaecologist Ernst Grafenberg who 'discovered' and unveiled the importance of this little miracle button of high eroticism in the mid-1940s.

Hers

If you have never found your G-spot or doubt its existence, then I would urge you to put this book down right now and potentially make a discovery that will revolutionise your sex life. Bold words – especially coming from a supposed sexpert. Situated on the upper wall of the vagina, it is like a tiny trigger which if pressed will release the most extraordinary waves of intense pleasure. And it can take a chance encounter to actually find it, either by your own fingers, those of your lover – or his penis if you're lucky – or with a vibrator shaped to reach the upper wall of the vagina. Try squatting down and inserting your index finger, to the second knuckle, in to a well-lubricated vagina and making a 'come over here' gesture towards the front of the vaginal wall. It's actually more like a zone than a spot, but feels a little rough like the surface of a walnut and although quite tiny – just the size of a pea – it actually expands to the size of a two-pence coin when stimulated.

Once you've established whether you've got one or not,

you need to discover whether you have one that gives you pleasure or just feels uncomfortable. Using a vibrator designed to stimulate the G-spot can be a revelation. Or use your fingers. Rather than pressing hard on the G-spot, which can be ultra-sensitive, make firm but gentle circling movements, stroking around the area, rather than directly over it.

During stimulation, the first sensation might be the need to go to the loo, possibly because the G-spot is on the front wall so your bladder is being pushed. You can check this out by making sure your bladder is empty first then seeing how it feels. The first couple of times it might be a bit odd, but many women say a little perseverance is more than worth it.

Depending on the size and exact location of your G-spot, you may or may not be able to feel stimulation during intercourse. You're most likely to feel something if you have your pelvis raised during the missionary position, sit on top of your partner where you have more control over the direction of your lover's penis or have sex doggy style, where the penis is in direct contact with your G-spot.

That's the good news. Unfortunately the not-so-good news is that it would appear that we don't all have one. In fact, while the research still continues, even including recent ultrasound scans to establish the existence of this thickened part of the vagina's upper wall, it would seem that only those women who can achieve a vaginal orgasm are likely to have a G-spot. Which, sadly, makes it less than one in three of us. Although even more recent research suggest that all women *do* have a G-spot, it's just that it's much less rich in nerve endings on many women. Given that most of us achieve wonderful orgasm through clitoral orgasm, it's definitely not worth worrying about if you find that you can't feel anything. However, recent research suggests that the sensitivity of this area increases with lower oestrogen levels, as the vaginal walls get thinner with a lack of oestrogen. So this is one instance where the peri (just before) or postmenopausal woman might just find that she's in an advantageous position.

If the latest research is correct and that all women are in possession of a G-spot (yay – thanks, latest researchers!) then make the most of yours by investing in a G-spot vibrator. With its curved tip, it is designed especially to maximise the G-spot area. Used with some lube and a firm rocking – rather than a thrusting – motion, hopefully you can start to recognise feelings that you never thought you'd experience. But be warned – it can feel very different from a clitoral orgasm the first few times that you do it. Apart from the feeling that you need to pee urgently (emptying your bladder first is a good idea . . .) it has an urgency about it that some women love and others definitely do not.

His

Men also have a G-spot, which is in fact their prostate gland, which is situated just below the bladder, surrounding the urethra. It's about the size of a walnut and its main function is to produce, store and secrete a clear fluid that constitutes up to one-third of the volume of semen.

When this particular gland is stimulated during vaginal or anal intercourse it can intensify a man's orgasm to the point of distraction. The prostate can be reached by inserting your finger or a vibrator and a gentle massage can produce a deep and highly erotic response for your partner.

Stimulation of the prostate gland can be either stroked whilst your lover is fully aroused and already fully erect or can be stimulated to increase his erections. Some men absolutely love having their G-spot stimulated, while others find it too uncomfortable or even distasteful, with its supposed connotations of gay sex.

However, it is a seriously sensitive and highly erogenous zone for a man and one of the few that are lurking inside his body, rather than hanging outside of it. Your man may just feel a little awkward at first, especially if his G-spot is as yet undiscovered, but do persevere, if your lover is willing. He may also indicate that he would like you to insert a finger into his anus, by spreading his legs wider during foreplay and lifting his pelvis slightly. So what should you do?

Make sure that you are both comfortable and your man has freshly showered and use a water-based lubricant to prevent friction. Smear your index finger with a good dollop of the lube and slowly insert it into his rectum. This is best done with fairly short nails, rather than long talons, as this could be unexpectedly sharp or painful in such a delicate area. Ask your man to relax and go with the strange feelings to begin with as much as possible. It may not be necessary to insert your whole finger to begin with as the most sensitive nerves are closer to the anal opening. Only when he is comfortable with your finger should you try and insert it further to seek out his prostate. Experiment a little by slowly inserting and pulling your finger out and see how he responds. Of course, he may not be new at this but if you are, go at the pace you feel comfortable with.

Once you have inserted your finger as far is it will go comfortably, slowly curl the tip upwards so that you are making a 'come here' movement. If you are in the correct place, this motion will gently stroke your man's prostate gland. Don't be too surprised if he comes just by you stroking this gland. Some men can and will. It's just a matter of finding out exactly what your man loves. Using a small bullet-shaped vibrator also works wonders, especially if you're a little squeamish about putting your finger inside your man's bottom!

A-spot

Another hot spot was accidentally discovered in the mid-90s (these scientific researchers must have been having a ball!) The A-spot is also clumsily known as the Anterior Fornix Erogenous Zone or AFE-zone, and is a patch of sensitive tissue located at the inner end of the vaginal canal, between your cervix and your bladder. If your clitoris is your mini-penis, then the A-spot is the female equivalent of the male prostate gland, or the male G-spot, see page 152. Direct stimulation of the A-spot can produce massive waves of orgasmic contractions and this can create rapid and copious amounts of vaginal lubrication. Researchers have found that this additional lubrication adds to the emotional and physical excitement of sex, and so women who have found and stimulated their A-spot, tended to have more frequent and intense orgasms, as well as being more likely to have multiple orgasms.

To find your A-spot, lubricate your vagina and slip your index and middle fingers inside your vagina, until you find your G-spot, if you have one (see page 149), and then continue upwards towards your cervix, which will feel firm but yielding (like the end of your nose). Somewhere around halfway between your cervix and your G-spot, you should find your A-spot, if you pull your fingers slowly back. Unlike the spongy G-spot, it feels harder and very sensitive to direct touch. But it's pretty far inside your vagina, so you or your lover will probably need extra long fingers to find it! You can also buy a long, thin probe-shaped AFE vibrator to discover this zone for yourself. If you want to stimulate your A-spot during sex, you'll find that doggy style, where the vaginal wall gets a direct hit from your lover's penis, is the easiest position to try.

U-spot

The U-spot is a small zone of highly sensitive tissue, found just above and on either side of the opening of your urethra. This is a relatively newly discovered erogenous zone, but one, which if gently stimulated with your man's tongue, finger or tip of his penis can cause a highly erotic response.

This is because it is situated so close to the urethra that it stretches during penetrative intercourse and it is believed that this stretching effect causes us to release the 'happy' hormone serotonin, making us especially aroused.

It's not the easiest hot spot to find, but if you can touch your urethra – the bit that you pee out of – you should find a small patch of sensitive tissue. Sometimes it's easier – and more pleasurable – to ask your partner to use the tip of his tongue to find and stimulate this, the tiniest of areas. Lubrication might help in this delicate process too. You might also feel the intensity of the U-spot if you spread your legs extra wide during penetrative intercourse and press yourself hard against your lover's penis, by thrusting your pelvis upwards a little and encouraging your partner to grind in firm circular motions, rather than just thrust into you.

Unlike the G-spot, which around only one in three of us are aware that we have, the little U-spot is more common and once you've found it, you may find that the kind of orgasm you have by pressing against it is quite a different rush to the one experienced during clitoral orgasm.

As I've mentioned, the three fun hot spots, G, A and U, are not always easy to find (though you can have a great time experimenting with different positions and expanding your sexual menu in the process) or comfortable to stimulate, and if you only ever manage to find and arouse your clitoris (and you must!) you'll still have the most rewarding sex life. These other hot spots are simply flourishes that can add a trick or two to your orgasmic repertoire.

Her orgasm

The female orgasm, as you've probably gathered by now, is a complex response – and has as much to do with your state of mind as it does your state of arousal.

Vaginal orgasm

The inner walls of the vagina are rich in nerve endings and for some women, around a third, it is possible to have a vaginal orgasm through penetrative intercourse, judicious use of fingers – yours or his – or using a vibrator. It is likely that there is some pressure of the clitoris going on too however, and it may be that you have a larger than 'normal' clitoris or that it is situated nearer the vaginal opening itself.

However it is possible to have a vaginal orgasm, without any stimulation of the clitoris, and it's often described as a wave of warmth and well-being, rather than the powerful roller-coaster of a clitoral orgasm. Any orgasm is good during sex and you shouldn't feel cheated if you tend to have vaginal, rather than clitoral, orgasms as a matter of course. Some women find that clitoral orgasms, with their deep intensity are a little 'full on' for their personal preference. It's also possible that you're one of the fortunate women (see page 149) who has a highly sensitive G-spot and you are able to achieve an orgasm through vaginal stimulation alone.

Clitoral orgasm

The clitoris is the best known of the female genital hot spots. It is located at the top of the vulva, just where your inner labia join at the top. The size of a small erect nipple, it is, in effect, your own mini-penis, becoming swollen, erect and engorged with blood, when stimulated, just like the male penis. It even has a small protective hood – also like the penis. Your clitoris contains over 8000 nerve fibres – making it the most sensitive spot, by far, on the entire female body. It has no reproductive function and simply exists for sexual pleasure. Lucky us! Recent research has shown that the clitoris consists of much more than simply the nerve-rich tip and that there is a shaft too, which runs down to the vaginal opening. This shaft consist of two stalks which in turn runs into two bulbs (yes, I know it's sound more like a sermon on gardening than a sex book at this stage, but bear with me . . .) which run down the area just outside the vaginal opening. All of this means that during pelvic thrusting there is usually a degree of clitoral stimulation, even when the tip itself is not touched directly.

Over two-thirds of women have orgasms only when they are stimulated clitorally, rather than – or as well as – vaginally. The sexual response cycle, as described on page 140, is the cycle of a clitoral rather than a vaginal orgasm. In fact, clitoral orgasm can be so intense and such a massive release of emotion and energy that it's not at all unusual to burst into tears – literally with relief – after an especially powerful one.

Blended orgasm

Blended orgasm is really what it says on the tin – an orgasm achieved through simultaneous vaginal (or G-spot) and clitoral stimulation. A blended orgasm requires different touches on two distinct body areas, and this extra effort naturally slows your lover down and helps him last longer. Additionally, men love it when a woman really loses herself in the powerful lust that a blended orgasm gives.

The best way to try and achieve a blended orgasm is to start by lying on your back comfortably and letting your body relax as much as possible. Ask your man to stroke your clitoris softly but firmly and as you become more aroused, encourage him to increase his pressure and speed until you're close to reaching your climax,

Once you're close to coming, ask your lover – or move his hand – away from your clitoris and move it to your vagina. As he massages your vagina and you become increasingly excited, get him to stimulate your clitoris with his other hand or use a vibrator while keeping his fingers inside your vagina. With practice, you'll start to feel an intense, almost overwhelming pulsating feeling with strong contractions, and you'll be on your way to the finale of a blended orgasm.

If you want to try this during penetrative intercourse, the best position is to adopt the doggy style. When you're on all fours and he's thrusting from behind, your lover's penis will naturally find your G-spot. Lean your upper body against the bed for support while reaching down and massaging your own clitoris as he thrusts. Or get him to use his own hand to rub your clitoris – he'll love this as he's in charge of both types of stimulation.

Multiple orgasms

Multiple orgasms, while being the stuff of male fantasy and porn films, are not quite as straightforward as the name implies. In simple terms, most people understand it to be two or more individual orgasms during a single sex session. While this is perfectly possible, and indeed desirable, the multi-orgasmic man or woman is more likely to peak and trough through the orgasmic experience, having two or three overlapping orgasms in succession. These orgasms generally increase in intensity with each subsequent wave and the finale is often one deserving of a major round of applause.

What actually happens to multi-orgasmic women is that with a technically adept and sensitive lover, particularly one with whom they are especially familiar, they can hover around stage two, the plateau phase, for a relatively long time. Their lover will take great pains to stimulate them in just the right amounts, in just the right places, in order that they hold off from the orgasmic phase itself and so feel wave after wave of arousal that brings them up to orgasm, but never quite reaching the resolution stage. If your man understands that direct clitoral or G-spot stimulation can bring you to a climax and if he is aware of the changes in your breathing, pulse rate and moans and groans as you near orgasm, he can move direct stimulation away from that area for a while.

Research has shown us that the kind of women who experience multiple orgasms – in fact, the kind of women who experience the most regular and fulfilling orgasms – tend to have the following five factors in common. If these don't apply to you, don't panic, they're just meant to give you a general picture of the kind of positive mental attitude that helps you lose inhibitions, relax and gives you the best chance of obtaining that climax.

1 Women who have learned about their bodies at an early age, investigated their clitoris and vagina in the mirror, before going on to enjoy regular masturbation in their everyday lives.
2 Women who enjoy giving and receiving oral sex.
3 Women who enjoy erotic fantasies, movies and books both on their own and with a partner.
4 Women who take an uninhibited and active role during sex, understanding what gives them pleasure and communicating this easily to their partner.
5 Women who form stable, satisfying relationships and understand the importance of regular sex within those relationships.

Ejaculation

Yes, it's not only guys that ejaculate during sexual arousal. Some women say they ejaculate when their G-spot is stimulated. Research has shown that approximately 10% of women expel between 9 and 900 millilitres of fluid from the urethra during arousal and orgasm. A group of scientists examined some of this ejaculatory fluid and discovered prostatic enzymes, fuelling the theory that the G-spot is the equivalent of the male prostate.

Whatever its composition – and some research says that it is pure urine – it can occur after a particularly powerful orgasm, as your Skene's glands that surround the urethral tube (the bit we pee through) secrete a thin, clear liquid when under extreme stimulation.

It feels different from the usual slipperiness of vaginal lubrication that comes from simple arousal, as it's more like a rush of fluid – though it can vary from a few drops to a small cupful. While ejaculation itself doesn't make any difference to the actual quality of a G-spot orgasm, you can stimulate ejaculation – if you've got a mind to – by making sure that you're up to speed on your pelvic floor exercises (see page 25) and using a G-spot vibrator to maximise your chances. Or just to see what it feels like!

His orgasm

The male orgasm is a less emotionally dependent creature than its female counterpart, but it's nevertheless equally complex in the physiological sense. As a man climaxes, his engorged reproductive glands spill their contents into his urethra and he'll ejaculate via a series of three to five spasmodic contractions, lasting just a few seconds. If he hasn't had sex or masturbated for a while, his orgasm – the emotional bit – will seem more intense and he'll produce more seminal fluid too. If he has recently masturbated, he might last longer before climaxing, but the feeling of orgasm might not feel so intense and the amount of semen produced is less.

Premature ejaculation

Premature ejaculation is when a man comes too quickly for either his or his partner's fulfilment. To a degree this is fairly subjective, as some men consider that they are premature ejaculators when 'only' having sex for fifteen minutes or more, whereas for others ejaculation can occur on penetrative entry, the first thrust, into their partner's vagina. As a general rule if you ejaculate within two minutes of penetration, this can be considered to be premature.

Around a third of men report that they experience premature ejaculation at some point in their sexually active lives. There are all sorts of temporary reasons why men encounter premature ejaculation including performance anxiety; lack of regular sex; stress; overindulgence in alcohol or recreational drugs or the fact that they have learned to be furtive during masturbation and to get the whole thing over with as quickly as possible.

Both the squeeze and the Jen-Mo techniques described on page 165 can help temporary premature ejaculation. If the problem persists, then don't be embarrassed to visit your GP. It's a common concern and a visit to a sex therapist or psychosexual counsellor can help you overcome what is frequently a temporary problem.

Delayed ejaculation

Delayed ejaculation, also known as retarded ejaculation, means that although you can maintain an erection all night if necessary, you find it very difficult or even impossible to ejaculate or have an orgasm. The cause of delayed or retarded ejaculation is often psychological.

Many men who suffer from this tend to have had a strict upbringing and are very controlled in their lives. It is especially common in highly successful men, who are at the top of their profession, in part by being emotionally detached from their private lives. They may have difficulty in showing emotions and in 'letting go'.

Other possible factors of delayed ejaculation include:

- fear of causing pregnancy
- fear that the vagina is dirty
- over-strict religious upbringing
- latent homosexuality
- guilt, especially if having an affair
- a physiological response to taking anti-depressants, recreational drugs or excess alcohol

Whatever the reason, if only mild it can be a bonus of course, but if severe or regular, it's worth seeing your GP.

Multiple orgasms

Men are also able to have multiple orgasms, but because they tend to need to rest immediately after climaxing (yup, that's why you tend to roll over and fall into a deep sleep after your orgasm) in order to regenerate your semen supplies, it's unlikely that you will be able to actually ejaculate more than once. Again it's in part down to your partner to help hold you back from full orgasm. One of the 'tricks' here is to use a Taoist technique called Jen-Mo, where your partner presses her finger on your perineum (the bit between your anus and your scrotum) as you near climax. This prevents the seminal fluid from travelling through the urethra. The pressure should be neither too soft nor too firm – just enough to stop the upward movement of the semen.

Another technique to prevent ejaculation is to get your partner to press her thumb, firmly but gently, just under the head of your penis – the squeeze technique. She shouldn't press too hard or you might find that you lose your erection altogether!

Men also have what's known as the non-ejaculatory orgasm – or the NEO. The NEO is like having an orgasm in the emotional sense, feeling it in your brain, but you inhibit ejaculation itself by contracting your own pubococcygeus muscle or PC muscle. You can flex and control this muscle by stopping the flow of urine, mid-pee – and the same principle works for ejaculation.

You can also help yourself become multi-orgasmic by mentally 'separating' your emotional pleasure of orgasm from the physiological release of ejaculation. Rather unsexily, this is best achieved by letting your mind drift away from sex itself on to rather more mundane matters like concentrating on the wallpaper pattern!

Multiple orgasms are not everybody's cup of tea, especially for men. One huge effort, one massive orgasm and rolling over to cuddle your partner before you go to sleep are more likely to be the order of the day!

Making it the best

Communication

One of the fundamental keys to great sex at any level, whether it's foreplay or wanting to achieve an orgasm – or a better, more exciting orgasm, is communication with your partner. Whether you tell your partner graphically and directly what feels good (and what doesn't) or indicate it with your gyrations and movements or push his hand to the various places you want him to touch, it's the best possible way to take the guess work out of reaching an orgasm.

But sometimes we're on the brink of orgasm and it just doesn't seem to be happening for us. This is where some serious dirty talk comes into its own. Judiciously using some swear words, along side some love talk, is often a lethal combination to bring you to the final stages of orgasm, so don't be afraid to encourage your partner to use them or simply initiate it yourself.

Making yours better: girls

Now you've understood the basics of actually achieving an orgasm, these tips will help you make it the best it can be:

- Prolong your foreplay. This encourages excitement and arousal and builds better, longer and more fulfilling orgasms.
- Make sure your partner understands how much you love having your breasts touched. Tell him about that invisible

'wire' that runs directly from your nipples downwards to your clitoris.

- Think like a belly dancer and swivel your pelvis during sex – the more you move your pelvis, the longer and more intense the sexual energy and control.

- Make sure your partner knows what makes you feel good and that you will probably take longer than him to climax. Make him feel in control and that your plateau hovering moments are fabulous in themselves rather an imminent indication of having an orgasm.

- Talk him through the feelings of having a clitoral orgasm and show him what you like – yes, it's the most highly sensitive area of our body but it's not an orgasmic flick-switch, it needs stimulating around the area, not a button to press directly on.

- Don't despair if you don't climax during every sex session or if they are not all peel-me-off-the-ceiling orgasms each and every time. Mood, stress levels and time factors all affect your ability to have an orgasm.

- Let yourself think sex. The mind is a powerful tool in having an orgasm so allow yours to wander freely through talking dirty, playing sexy music, watching a porn movie, having a fantasy or whatever it is that makes the mood just right for you.

- Make a note on the calendar or in your diary of your 'hot' days. Many women find that there are days, in your ovulation cycle, when you feel more aroused than others and so it's easier to orgasm.

Making yours better: guys

- Don't fret about coming too quickly, it will make the likelihood greater. Think about something banal for a moment or two, or encourage your partner to use one of the holding techniques recommended on page 165.

- Masturbate an hour or two before sex to keep that supply of semen building up and you'll feel less likely to climax too quickly.

- Having a quickie to start with, and climaxing quickly, will take the urgency out of a subsequent sex session and enable you to have a less physically pressured orgasm.

- Masturbate in front of your partner. Let her see exactly how you give yourself a hand job and the speed, rhythm and position that you prefer. Your partner can then take over and you can report back on her progress via your appreciative moans and groans.

- If you feel that you're going to climax fairly soon, switch to oral sex or something else for a while, to defuse the moment.

- Focus on the sensation and how good it's making you feel rather than how quickly you're going to climax – it puts you in a more relaxed state of mind.

- Watch your alcohol intake – as well as decreasing your chances of having and maintaining an erection, alcohol also numbs and represses your bodily functions, making it tougher to focus on sustaining that erection and holding off your climax.

- Use lubricant to make the whole process more slippery and more arousing for both of you.

THE LONGEST ORGASM – THE ESO TECHNIQUE

Given that the average female orgasm actually only lasts up to around 15 seconds at best – even if the getting there took much, much longer – what would it feel like if you could have an orgasm that lasted up to 30 *minutes*? This has been the bold claim of two sexperts in America, Alan and Donna Brauer, who have developed a programme called the Extended Sexual Orgasms technique (ESO Technique). If followed correctly with your partner, and it can be quite a demand, they have shown that all women are potentially capable of experiencing a continuous, deeply intense orgasm lasting at *least* 30 minutes. And if this weren't enough, you can be reminded of your long-drawn-out pleasure by feeling sporadic deep contractions up to 24 hours later too.

Step One: On Your Own

- **Think positively about sex.** And allow yourself the indulgence of 'me time'. Most of us, according to the sexologists, resist rather than embrace pleasure, so you need to do some 'cognitive restructuring'. Keep thinking that you're having a fabulous time rather than worrying about whether you've bought enough milk for the weekend.
- **Practise your Kegel pelvic floor exercises.** This involves squeezing, holding, and then releasing the same muscles that you use to stop yourself mid-flow while peeing. See page 25 for more information on how to exercise your pelvic floor muscles.
- **Masturbate more regularly.** Get to know and practice which strokes, speed, pressure and rhythms suit you best.

Step Two: With Your Partner

- You need to lie down while your partner sits or kneels cross-legged beside you or in between your legs and applies some lubricant to the whole of your vagina and perineum (the skin between your vagina and anus). Then he should lightly stroke and tease your genitals for at least five minutes, but he's not allowed to stimulate your clitoris and the inside of your vagina.

- He should then begin to stimulate your clitoris by drawing slow and steady circular movements around your clitoris, with his index finger, travelling around it once per second. At the same time, you should tell him exactly what pressure and rhythm feels good for you.

- As he continues to stimulate your clitoris, you start doing your pelvic floor squeezes as you breathe deeply from your stomach, rather than shallow breathing from your stomach. If this is all going to plan, your orgasm shouldn't be far away now.

- As you feel you're about to come, your partner should concentrate, by watching and feeling for regular two-second contractions in your genital area, which indicate that you're about to orgasm. Once these contractions start, he needs to stop stimulating the clitoris and immediately move to stroking the inner vaginal walls. Using his fingers, he can either push them in and out, or sweep them in circles, slowly and steadily, in and out of your vaginal entrance.

- After you've had your orgasm, he'll feel the vagina start to draw back - the point when most orgasms subside as you start to come down. But in ESO, the aim is to prolong these

- contractions, so your partner should keep his fingers inside your vagina, stroking you gently until you indicate that you want him to apply more pressure and more frequency. This should set off another series of contractions and he should carry on stimulating the inner walls of the vagina.
- The moment that he feels a pause in the pulsating, he should move quickly back to stroking the clitoris as before. If he continues to steadily circle the clitoris, this should trigger even more contractions - at which point he moves back to stimulating inside the vagina again. He then continues switching back and forth from vaginal to clitoral stimulation until your contractions occur every one to five seconds.
- After doing this for 15 minutes, the vagina will begin to draw away less and less and the contractions start to become continuous. When the vagina pushes out in a continual wave-like motion, you're in the final phase. He now gets into a position where he can use both hands to stimulate the clitoris and the vagina simultaneously. The result should be an amazing wave after wave of multiple orgasms.

Simultaneous orgasm

It just seems so *fair* to have simultaneous orgasms. After all, you're both putting in plenty of effort and wouldn't it be good – and romantic – if you could both climax at exactly the same time. Well, yes it would, of course, and it's certainly achievable – just not nearly so common as the sexually 'airbrushed' world of movies would have us believe. Having an orgasm is essentially a selfish moment in time – it's an intense concentration of self-pleasure and complete relaxation, so it can be a bit off-putting to have to pay too much attention to whether your partner is doing exactly the same thing at exactly the same time. And for men it's almost impossible, because once their orgasm has begun there's no going back. Some women, on the brink of orgasm, do find that their partner makes the kind of 'Oh my god, I'm coming noises' and thrusts very deeply during the final phases, so much so that this alone brings their excitement levels to their own orgasm.

Because women take so much longer to climax than men, the only way you'll be likely to manage the unison of climaxing simultaneously is for your partner to make sure that you get plenty of foreplay so that you're sufficiently aroused and in the plateau phase before you actually have penetrative sex. And that takes plenty of pleasurable practice, but when it does happen there is something deliciously bonding and romantic about both coming together at the same moment.

MORE ORGASMS, MORE OFTEN

For some women, the detail of where – and how – they are having an orgasm is simply too much information. You have them and they feel good and the technical detail isn't relevant. So, what do you do if you just want to be sure of having that 'Martini' orgasm, anyhow, any place and anywhere? Let's look at how you can introduce a little climactic variety in the five basic positions, listed in chapter 4.

YOU'RE ON YOUR WAY TO BEING SEXY IF . . .

- **Man on top: the missionary position**
  Instead of your lover doing the traditional pounding and thrusting motion, try grinding against his pelvis and moving back and forth in circular motions. It gives as much chance as possible to ensure that the whole of the vulva is stimulated as much as possible.

- **Woman on top: the cowgirl**
  As you've got the most control in this position, it's easier to have ownership of your own orgasm. You can squeeze and tighten your vagina around your lover's penis as you rock to and fro. You can also lean in forwards and flatter, again increasing your chance of clitoral orgasm.

- **Rear-entry sex: doggy style**
  This is one of the easiest positions in which to have an orgasm, as there is plenty of stimulation of the front vaginal wall, home of the G- and A-spots. You can also try lifting your bottom higher during this position, maximising the chances of your lover's penis getting a direct hit at the vaginal front wall. Your partner can also give you extra clitoral stimulation in this position.

- **Side by side: spooning**
  This is a fairly languid, unhurried affair so achieving an orgasm can be more difficult this way. The key to a great orgasm in the spooning position, where it's rear entry while lying side by side, is to make sure that your partner is giving you plenty of clitoral stimulation while

penetrating you. If you want more control, take over and masturbate your clitoris to bring you to a climax in your own way. Or use a vibrator against your clitoris as you're having sex.

- **The quickie**
  The urgent, spontaneous need of a quickie is often enough to bring you to a climax pretty quickly, however and wherever it's taking place. Make sure you are really in the mood by talking or texting dirty just beforehand so there's plenty of mental build up. And wear the kind of clothes and underwear that can be removed quickly – your orgasm ability will deflate if there are lots of fastenings and zips to get off quickly!

While orgasm is considered by many to be the nirvana of great sex, it's your own imagination that fuels truly great sex. And what better way to fuel your imagination, than to act out role play, indulge in a little fantasy or lose yourself with the kind of sex toy that will give you maximum pleasure whether flying solo or shared with a partner.

7 Sex Games: Fantasies, Role Play, Games and Toys

Fantasies, dressing up and playing with sex toys. Sleazy, smutty, shameful thoughts to be banished to the darkest recesses of your guilty mind? Or lust-filled, imaginative, fun and joyous sex shared with someone you trust with your most intimate thoughts?

No prizes for guessing where I stand on this one. Being able to share your deepest desires and fantasies with your partner should be liberating and exciting, not embarrassing, or disgusting or abnormal. Whatever goes on privately between two consenting adults should be considered normal. You may not want to do everything your partner suggests – or vice versa – but openness, honesty and being sexually adventurous is key to a passionate, fulfilling sex life, especially in a long-term relationship.

So what holds us back from trying something new and different? Basically it's down to fear. Fear of our bodies, losing control, looking ridiculous or the sheer rawness of this level of intimacy feeling just too intimidating. Add to this the sense that using what used to be referred to as sex 'aids' – thankfully now just known as sex toys – had connotations of being both sleazy and needing some sort of assistance or help with your sex life, means that a lot of people just don't bother to explore this fun-filled side of their sex lives.

I have divided this chapter up into fantasies, role play, games and toys. It's a slightly artificial division as many sexual fantasies do involve dressing up and role play and both fantasies and role play can easily involve sex toys, for example. But broadly speaking, fantasies are those imaginings going on in our heads – the sort of 'naughty' or wild daydreams that help excite us both during sex and while we're simply feeling distracted – whether travelling on the bus to work or just watching TV, with or without our partner. Role play is generally dressing up in costumes, using props or adlibbing our way through a particular sexual scenario – so it's anchored more in real time than in our fantasy world. Games are an even more specialist form of role play with proper 'instructions', a staged process and a relatively predictable outcome – just like playing any other sort of game. And with the plethora of sex toys available out there, I have simply gone through what each type of toy is actually meant to do, how to use them and those that I personally rate and recommend.

Sex Fantasies

The two questions that I get asked most frequently, regarding sexual fantasies, are 'Is it OK to fantasise *during* sex?' and 'What happens when a fantasy develops into the real thing?' The first question is easy enough to answer, as absolutely 'yes' is my answer and you'll discover why as you read further.

The second question however, is much more of a tough call. Firstly, it is often one partner, more than the other, who is driving a fantasy to become a reality and this can cause a serious imbalance in a relationship, if what started as an innocent-enough fantasy designed to fuel sexual desire and fun, becomes a pressurised situation to turn that fantasy into real time. Secondly, there are absolutely no boundaries in the fantasy world, whether you choose to share these with your partner or not, yet the reality can be disappointing at best and at worst, be a fatal blow to a relationship or permanently damage your own self-esteem. Much of the fallout of your special daydreams becoming reality is down to the fantasy itself. Wanting and having an erotic massage is quite different to fancying and then arranging a threesome, for example. Many of your reactions to 'doing it for real' depends on your own confidence to explore further as a couple, the strength and durability of your relationship and the ability to deal with any unforeseen consequences in an honest and straightforward way. Which is a very long way of saying that the more complex fantasies should be appreciated for simply being that – a fantasy, a daydream and tool to stimulate you physically and emotionally during sex – unless you and your partner are both of exactly the same mind, with no pressure from one or the other, and can weigh up the potential emotional fallout in a mature and open way and accept that it undoubtedly *will* have some effect on your relationship, albeit not necessarily in a disastrous way.

Using your imagination

The brain, as you will have gathered by now, is a pretty amazing organ when it comes to having great sex. Without the emotional response all those nerve endings, all over our skin, when touched, would simply feel like, er, touch. And not very sexy touch at that – more like a doctor checking a reflex reaction than a delicious lover awakening you into arousal. Even if you've run the course (lucky you!) of every sexual position described in this book, your imagination is still limitless. Whether you're with a partner or single, a virgin or an experienced lover, there can be no one out there who hasn't had some tingling of arousal by letting their mind wander to a sexual fantasy whether it's triggered by something you're reading in a book or magazine, an advert, watching a movie or TV or the simple pleasure of a cool breeze on a summer's day.

There's absolutely no guilt in having these fantasies. If you're single, your imagination is your sexual playground. And if you're in a relationship, you can feel that lustful, naughty edge that fantasy gives you. As I've mentioned, most – but not all – fantasies are best left in your head. They are forbidden pleasures in the main, especially the more explicit ones, with no rules. But although you might feel that some of them are 'inappropriate' – sleeping with a person of the same sex or wanting to be taken by force – these are healthy fantasies that allow our imagination to roam freely and be curious about the world around us. They do not mean that we want literally a homosexual affair or to be raped. Pinning down your assistant over the boardroom table and spreading her legs wide before announcing that you're going to give her the time of her life is a sexy moment of distraction during a mundane working day. In reality you know that you'll be frogmarched out of the building, out of your job and probably in court for sexual harassment before you can say it was only a fantasy. In fact, sex therapists are generally agreed that providing you can clearly distinguish between fantasy and reality and fully acknowledge the real-time consequences of real-time actions, sexual fantasies are a brilliant and indulgent way of letting off imaginary steam without recourse to anything actually immoral or illegal.

Many of us start having fantasies in our childhood. I didn't even know what sex really was when I wanted the pop star David Cassidy to take me in his arms and consume me in some way. I didn't want to marry him – I just wanted him, all of him. I was a pre-teen and this gorgeous, floppy-haired boy was my secret longing. The closest I got, of course, was wearing out the paper lips of my poster boy on my bedroom wall as I kissed his image before I went to bed! Then when I moved onto some other pin-up pop star, he was torn down and replaced by my new desire. And so it is with most of us. Our fantasies evolve in time – one minute we can't wait to deflower a cute looking schoolboy, the next minute we're after a sexy older guy to impart a little sexual wisdom. And the truth is most of us fantasise about things that we'd hate to happen in reality – do you really want to watch the pizza delivery boy making out with your girlfriend? – but it's a perfect release to our normal, day-to-day lives and allows our libidos to soar. In fact, the more you fantasise, the higher your sex drive probably is. Fantasies are free, available anywhere at any time, can be turned on and off at will and banish all real-life intrusions, from wobbly love handles to worrying about paying the mortgage, into another world. What's not to like?

Research shows that around 90% of us fantasise at some point when we're having sex with a partner. Where do we go when we close our eyes or when we're making love facing away from our partner? Add to that 90%, the fact that a similar number of people fantasise each and every time that they masturbate and you have 100% of sexually active people fantasising at some time or another. Which is encouraging news because the same research shows that those people who do regularly fantasise have more fulfilling sex lives than their less imaginative counterparts.

How to get what you want

So, given that all these fantasies are healthy for our sex lives and to be encouraged and being honest, upfront and communicative with your partner is one of the best ways to a satisfying sex life, is it OK to tell your partner the details about your own fantasies? Well, it's perhaps the one area of our sexual lives where it's definitely best to proceed with caution. Revealing your own personal fantasies can send your sex life through the roof. It can make it sizzle with variety and excitement. Unfortunately, admitting your fantasies can also destroy your relationship. If your partner doesn't share your enthusiasm for a particular fantasy, it can make him or her feel inadequate, insecure and jealous. This is where a clear definition between role play and fantasy is needed. Fantasies are essentially private thoughts, whereas role play is a shared affair where the two of you can participate together in playing out a particular scenario. Unless you know your partner very well and can accurately gauge their reactions, my advice is to keep fantasies reasonably private. Even more so if it involves someone you actually know. Admitting that you fancy a celebrity, who you are very unlikely to meet, is very different to revealing that you'd like to have sex doggy style, strapped into a gimp suit, with your partner's best friend.

But if you do want to reveal your fantasy, or indeed want to consider acting it out role-play style, then like anything slightly 'delicate' – who's going to whose parents for Christmas dinner or suggesting that your partner's personal habits don't quite pass muster – you need to choose your moment wisely. You need to find a moment that's relaxed, private and intimate. Maybe tell your partner that you had an amazing dream last night (OK, small white lie, it is a dream, just a day version) where something incredibly sexy and surprising happened. See if they react positively to that before going any further. Or ask them if they have any special fantasies – but be prepared for an answer that you might not have wanted or anticipated. Take it a step at a time – fantasies are always easier to act out if you both share a common goal. If his fantasy is to have his testicles massaged with baby oil and yours is to be spit roasted by the entire England football team, then it might be better to keep them as private thoughts after all.

Top 10 female fantasies

So what are the top 10 female sex fantasies? While all of us have individual fantasies, fuelled by our own imaginations, there are recurring themes in the most common female fantasies.

1 Sex with another man other than your partner

This is perhaps the most common female sexual fantasy of all, especially if you've had few partners in your life or have been with someone a long time. This could be a stranger, a celebrity, a friend or more often than not a past lover. If you look back in your life, you might find that however much you love your current partner or however fabulous he is in bed, the actual sex that you had with someone else was technically better. This is reassuring and normal. Psychologically, we tend to go for a long-term partner that has a number of attributes that we're looking for, whether that's kindness and consideration, reliability and honesty, intelligence or sense of humour – whatever it is as individuals that we seek. If he also happens to be the hottest man that you have ever had sex with then you have truly hit the jackpot – most of us tend to accept the sex is wonderful, but not necessarily the best ever.

2 **Something 'naughty' and new**
Our definition of naughty has a lot to do with the way
we were brought up. For some women, having sex with
the lights on would seem fairly outrageous while for
others being taken by force by half a dozen prisoners on
the run in the back of a filthy van would get them going.
It's all about fantasising about something that you have
never done before, especially if it's something that you
were brought up to believe wasn't 'nice' or was never
to be discussed. Being tied up, watching others have
sex and having a threesome are all healthy examples of
being naughty.

3 **Sex with another woman**
There is something hugely appealing about fantasising
about having sex with another woman. They have lovely
soft, fulsome bodies and breasts and vaginas just like us.
And there's always the thought that it's titillating to a lot
of men to imagine us having sex with another woman. It
doesn't feel like we're being unfaithful, both because they
are a woman rather than another man and it's all in our
heads anyway. But we know what feels good when our
breasts are touched in the right way, when oral sex is done
perfectly and how we like to be kissed. So isn't it all more
likely to be fulfilling if another women with the same bits
as us could have a go too? Or we can bask in the fantasy
that we'd know exactly how to give great oral sex and
no wrist ache either. And unlike a straight man fancying
another man, it's somehow a whole lot more acceptable.

4 **Having sex against our will**

I baulk at using the word 'rape' with all it's premise of violation and potentially devastating consequences, but basically many women do have fantasies about being taken against their will and forced into having sex by someone that they wouldn't choose to find sexy in the real world. Let's call it safe rape. A slightly silly phrase, but while our fantasies about having sex against our will are usually passionate and dramatic, they are rarely disgusting or unpleasant. It's usually the big burly man, taking us on command and is often a way of relinquishing the control that we choose to have – or are obliged to adopt – in our real lives.

Alternatively, if we don't have controlling positions in our real lives or feel that we would like to assume more, professionally or personally, fantasising about being the dominant partner and forcing a man to have sex with us is a way of releasing those feelings in a safe and managed way.

5 **Sex with a stranger**

The fantasy of sex with a stranger is raw, unadulterated sex. Unsullied by the burdens of everyday life and unfettered by the emotional demands of a relationship, this is pure no-strings-attached sex. You can be as naughty as you like and say and do as you please. You can take over the reins or let him have complete control.

6 **Playing the prostitute**

Whatever your actual views on men paying for sex, playing the role of a prostitute is another common female fantasy. The very act of being paid for sex means that you are being rewarded for looking gorgeous and someone finding you sexy. Very often this fantasy takes place in a street or a private club where men have the choice of the women that they want to pay for – and you are the chosen one, deemed sexier than all the others. It's also a chance to fantasise about wearing revealing, tight and seriously suggestive clothes and make-up.

7 Being tied up and out of control

Being tied up or harnessed to a bed or a chair where you have little chance to move and you are completely at the mercy of a man is the secret fantasy of many women. It allows you to be naughty and enjoy teasing, spanking and whipping without being able to do anything about it. If you feel any guilt about the pleasures of S & M in the real world, your out of control fantasy will allow you to indulge it, guilt-free.

8 Mills & Boon world

A gentle and traditional fantasy, this is the type of escapism found in old-fashioned romantic novels. It's the dishy doctors and heaving bosom combo, often combined with a lot of eye contact, eyelash fluttering and deep sighs. Or it could be a moonlit walk, hand in hand with a delicious dark, brooding man who only has eyes for you, along a perfect, soft sandy beach. It's a lovely and romantic form of escapism and one fantasy that many women, understandably, are happy to confess to.

9   Sex with a work colleague

However senior you are at work or however busy, I suspect that there isn't one of us who hasn't daydreamed about what a work colleague might be like in bed. What would he be like giving us great oral sex under the desk? We spend a lot of time, in a non-sexual way, with male colleagues and this fantasy expresses a natural curiosity about parts of their other lives that we don't have access to and what they might look like with their clothes off.

10 Sex with your current partner

A reassuring fantasy that many of us indulge in. As I mentioned it's incredibly healthy to have sexual fantasies and women who do have them tend to have a more satisfying sex life. Fantasising about what you would like your partner to do to you – or what you would like to do to him – when you next see him or when you're actually having sex with him, keeps your sex life and libido fresh and vital.

Top 10 male fantasies

Men's sex fantasies tend not to be that different from those of women, although they can tend to be more carnal than romantic. They often involve quite specific 'naughty' things like anal or oral sex, rather than just something that they might feel they don't feel ready to indulge in real life.

1   Sex with another woman other than your partner

The most common and most simple male sex fantasy. It's the grass-is-greener-on-the-other-side scenario. Only you can indulge in it without any consequences or fallout from your current partner. You might fantasise about a woman with huge breasts, a forbidden woman like your partner's sister or a prostitute or even a virgin that you can seduce and teach all things sexual to last them a lifetime . . .

2 **Sex with their current partner**
Just like women, this is a reassuringly common fantasy. You daydream about what you're going to do to her when you next see her or what you've already done, replayed over in your mind. It's also a gratifying fantasy, because unless you are fantasising about something you know or anticipate your partner will hate, the chances are you can fulfil this one with relative ease!

3 **Sex with a work colleague**
It might be your super-efficient, powerful female boss or it might be the shy assistant from accounts who looks like butter wouldn't melt in her mouth. But you will most definitely have fantasised about a work colleague at some point in your job and the chances are high that you probably regularly drift off into the idea of giving that boss a good 'seeing to' over the boardroom table or relish watching the demure assistant letting her hair down, sexually speaking.

4 **Sex with a stranger**
There's something very appealing about having anonymous sex with a stranger. You might fantasise about catching someone's eye in a hotel bar and without speaking a word,

you give her a signal and she follows you up to your hotel bedroom. Or it might be a woman you see on a regular train journey and you let your eyes and mind wander to her breasts and mouth, wondering what she'd be like giving you oral sex.

5 **Watching and being watched during sex**
Watching another couple have sex, also known as voyeurism, is a common fantasy because sex is essentially a private affair and while you might joke with your mates in the pub about how much – or how little – sex you're getting, the truth is we are all curious about just how other people have sex. Is it the same as you? For this reason, you might fantasise about watching someone you know having sex, especially a man whose 'performance' you might be curious about. Being watched while having sex, or exhibitionism, is usually a show-off fantasy. You want to share just how adept you are at making love, especially if another woman is watching, and of course, being a fantasy your sexual skills naturally rival that of the hottest porn star on the planet!

6 **Anal sex**
I once saw a very funny comedian who was sending up man's desire for anal sex. Why would they want to go to that dry and dirty place, when there's a warm, moist more yielding place just adjacent? It made the women laugh out loud, but most of the men squirmed with uncomfortable acknowledgement. Many men love the anal sex fantasy, because it's such a forbidden area and because it's such a highly erotic zone on their own body.

7 Bondage

Bondage is another classic male fantasy. Only this is usually where you take control and tie up your partner, rather than being tied up yourself. Which is good news, given that women usually want to be tied up themselves! Bondage fantasies are dreams involving power and control. In the twenty-first century, where some men feel that their alpha male masculinity is under threat, this fantasy has become ever more common. Inflicting pain, through whipping and spanking is another part of the bondage fantasy, as it's the ultimate control and relates to the pain–pleasure axis that are never very far apart during S & M sex.

8 Oral sex

Men generally have major fantasies about being given – rather than giving – oral sex. And in your fantasies, the woman will be doing it because *she* finds it so pleasurable, and not just to give you pleasure. She will fall upon your penis with relish and unabated desire, showering your manhood with compliments and consume your penis with utmost delight, while swallowing your semen with the kind of ecstasy it so rightly deserves.

9 Threesomes

Many men fantasise about their partner getting it on with another woman while they watch or, even better, join in. Threesome fantasises are nearly always two women and you (rarely two men) and usually involve your partner and another woman who you probably know. In your fantasies you'll not only be getting off on watching your partner drown in pleasure with this other woman, you'll also be able to satisfy them both in a way that they have never experienced before. These dreams are sometimes indicators of your doubts that you are in fact actually managing to fulfil your own partner – never mind another woman too – and sometimes an 'acceptable' way of bringing that other, forbidden woman, into your sex life.

10 Being seduced by an older woman

A lot of younger men want a fast track to sexual experience without the commitment of a relationship first. The older-woman scenario provides perfect fodder for this fantasy. A woman who has wisdom, bags of sexual expertise, is old enough to know what she wants and not be too modest to go for it and who can see that a proper relationship would be out of the question, due to the age gap is the perfect solution. For some men, this was an early sexual fantasy – often fancying your best mate's mum or a teacher at school – and one that you enjoy returning to.

Dreamtime or real time?

There are some fantasies that are really simple desires – the things that you'd like to do with your partner, aren't too 'outrageous' and once you've taken the first steps to sharing them, will probably become a pleasurable reality for you. And there are others, which if given airtime in the real world, could rock your relationship to the core. These are some other fantasies that you might indulge in, in no particular order – other than that they range from the relatively easy to share and fulfil to the fantasies best left in the privacy of your imagination.

Ice play

Remember that delicious sensation of an ice cube melting on your body on a really hot day? Amazingly cool relief from the sun; a slightly shocking feeling but actually it was way too cold. That sensation is a fairly mild form of pain/pleasure syndrome, so beloved of BDSM (Bondage, Domination, Submission and Masochism) enthusiasts, but playing with ice can be fun.

When things steam up in the bedroom or you're in a secluded, but public place take a small ice cube and gently use your finger to trace a pattern over your partner's body. Glide the ice across their nipples, down towards their tummy and then tease a little between their thighs. If you're in a little more seclusion, take the ice cube in your mouth and do the same thing. Let your tongue lap away the droplets formed by the melting ice. You can also use an ice cube to numb up your lover's labia, which gives an amazing feeling especially if aroused. If your man can bear it, and the sensation is not too acute, you can also use a slightly melted ice cube to stroke over his perineum and anal opening. If all this seems just too frosty, simply sucking an ice cube also makes your mouth lovely and cold when you give your partner oral sex.

Wax play

Like ice play, wax play has that naughty but nice element, only it has the added bonus of being slightly dangerous – so do take care when using melted candles. Plain white candles are the best for wax play, as they burn at the lowest temperature. Beeswax candles are definitely to be avoided – they can cause severe burning. If in doubt, test a few drops of wax on your own skin before trying it out on your partner. Some sex-toy companies also produce special massage candles, which burn at low temperatures, and are designed for wax play.

So what do you do with this sort of pain play? You could try blindfolding your partner and letting some drops of wax fall on random parts of their body. It's best to keep to the tummy or their back – and avoid the genitals at all costs; this is most definitely not an area for wax play!

If you find you enjoy playing out this fantasy, your partner may hate it, so proceed with caution both in safety and sympathetic terms – peeling it away from the skin can also produce an intense sensation that some couples like.

Sex with a celebrity

This was probably one of your earliest fantasies. Along with fancying the boy or girl next door, or the person who sat next to you at school, most of us had the hots for a pop star or a movie star. They are unreal, perfect (especially in an age of retouched photography) always immaculately turned out, powerful and successful. A heady brew. Celebrities always seem to lead a charmed life and are inevitably more interesting and exciting than our current, decent, but not-that-exciting partner. In reality, they probably have the same issues as the rest of us and bear scant resemblance to the person that their PR machine wants us to think that they are. But they're cute, sexy and you're never going to meet them. So they can't judge you either. Fantasise away . . .

Watching porn

Lots of men fantasise about watching porn with their partner and truth is that they are pleasantly surprised by the reaction – lots of women love watching porn as much as men and find it a real turn-on. But how do you suggest this in the first place and what kind of thing should you watch?

If you're a guy, used to watching porn to masturbate, you need to take a little care over your first foray into watching porn with your partner. You might be used to seeing the perfectly formed pink hairless vaginas, over-inflated breasts and platinum hair extensions so beloved by the porn industry, but the chances are that your partner might feel a bit insecure the first time she sees them. My feeling is to go for 'natural', fairly soft porn, where the girls look like proper girls and no surgical enhancements are allowed. Or start with a mainstream movie that has some hot sex in it or classic sex films that can be rented at your local DVD store. Or go online and do a little research into what kind of porn you could be buying into. As a rule of thumb, anything directed by a woman is usually a little softer than those movies made by men! This is a progressive fantasy – start gentle and move on up to the harder stuff at a pace that suits you both.

Watching porn together can be good fun. It's exciting, it's naughty and it can show you things visually that you might want to have a go at. But some porn is so awful (don't expect anything but the flimsiest of plotlines) that you may well find yourself giggling nervously and finding it hugely unsexy.

The thing to remember with watching porn movies is that they are not meant to be watched, with a family bucket of popcorn in your laps and your mind on the plotline. They should be there in the background to excite you while you masturbate together, or in turn, or take turns to give each other oral sex while your partner watches the film. If you both want to watch the movie together, get in a position that allows you to have sex as well as both watching the TV – doggy style or woman on top, facing away from your lover, both work well.

Making porn

Instead of watching porn with your partner, how about making your own movie instead? Men, especially, love the idea of starring in their own porn movie. Part of the fun is planning and then acting out the movie on your very own video cam or camera. This a harmless, natural fantasy – and one that adds a lot of spice to a couple's sex life as they can get an extra turn-on, by enjoying watching it afterwards. One word of warning, especially for women – if you are going to make a tape, keep it in a safe place. Or delete it afterwards. Some men love to show the movie to their mates after a few drinks – it's that showing off thing that makes him look like a hot stud muffin!

Spanking

I cover the serious side of spanking on page 233 (well, the kind of spanking that needs real props like paddles and whips). But spanking is the kind of fantasy that involves domination (as the spanker) or submission (as the one being spanked). And it's a contentious fantasy because it implies either wanting to be hurt or wanting to hurt someone you care for. And why would you want to do that to your lover? Men especially find the whole spanking issue a bit of a conundrum as it can seem degrading to their partner even if she tells them that she likes it or wants them to do it! So mix the pain/pleasure principle up with some guilt about the role men and women adopt in 'civilised' society and you've got a great recipe for the forbidden pleasure that is the spanking fantasy . . .

Sex with a virgin

Fantasising about deflowering a virgin is common for both men and women. It's all about power, dominance and imparting your sexual wisdom to an innocent party so that they can go out into the world and use that wonderful experience to share with other lovers. We also enjoy fantasises about being deflowered. Playing the innocent virgin, shy and coy and longing to be taught the sexual ways of the world, is very appealing, especially if our own first time wasn't quite the romantic novel scenario of being swept off our feet by a gorgeous, confident lover with the sexual prowess and sensitivity of a Hollywood movie star. Which let's face it, is a pretty unlikely scenario in the real world.

But this is a fantasy that you can play out with your lover. As a woman, you can be the seducer by wearing a sexy little outfit of pencil skirt, sharp white blouse teasingly undone to your cleavage and killer heels. You could play any sort of role play where you're the dominant partner – a boss interviewing him for a job or perhaps he's a young boy just looking to do a spot of gardening for you. Or you can reverse roles where, you are the sweet innocent, wearing a prim little blouse, buttoned to the neck or a schoolgirl outfit and your partner is your teacher or boss. There's more on the role playing out of fantasies on page 198.

Threesomes

Now we're definitely entering better-kept-to-a-dream territory. Most men and many women have a threesome fantasy – if you enjoy sex, why wouldn't you want two people pleasuring you simultaneously? And what guy doesn't want to watch two women pleasuring each other? It's hot, exciting and very risqué. But it's also very risky to a relationship. Truth is, as much as your man might fantasise, or even suggest, a threesome to you, he would probably prefer a threesome where neither of the two women (and it's nearly always two women!) are his partner. It's a whole lot less complicated that way.

Having a threesome, or a *ménage à trois*, can open up a Pandora's box of emotions that can be very hard to deal with after the fun is over. There's jealousy to deal with, a lack of trust, resentment as well as inadequacy – why weren't you 'good' enough on your own in the first place?

When we're young and at college after a few too many drinks or a bit stoned, a threesome can seem like an uncomplicated laugh. The sort of sexual experimentation that seems like harmless fun and part of growing up. But when we're in any kind of a settled relationship, however wild our sex lives might be, it really can threaten the stability of that relationship. It's an instance where the fantasy is generally much better than the reality. It can make you feel self-conscious, under pressure to perform but most importantly it leaves a bitter taste in the mouth, unless – which in itself is rare – you're both absolutely up for it, happy with emotionless sex and strong enough to deal with the guilt, jealousy and blame that so often follows on.

But although I really think (hey, it's just an opinion – albeit one shared by most sexperts) that it's not a great idea to go through with a threesome in real time, there will be those of you out there determined to have a go, so if you must, these are my five basic rules you should be following.

1 Agree on the male to female combo and who should be involved. This is one instance where strangers are a much better option than friends. There are plenty of swinging options on Internet sites where you can keep it relatively anonymous and use a hotel room or an organised club, rather than take it into your own bedroom. And if you're finding your third person online, meet first to discuss what you want out of the situation. And use your instincts to walk away if there's anything remotely dodgy about it or if you just don't see the sexual chemistry working.

2 Agree on what's allowed and what isn't it. Don't feel that discussing it first somehow diminishes any of the excitement you're going to enjoy. It's absolutely imperative

that you discuss what is and what isn't allowed, who is allowed to do what to whom and if one of you wants to stop at any point, you agree to both stop. You both have to be comfortable with each other's needs and respect each other's limits. Threesomes don't have to involve penetrative sex for example – the limits just need to be agreed by all parties beforehand.

3 Always use a condom. Or a number of condoms, making sure that you change them between partners.

4 Make sure your partner is key to the threesome and this is a joint activity with your partner being the focus of attention, not the third party. However much the other person arouses you, you're going home as a couple.

5 Don't be too greedy (given that threesomes are pretty much all about greed). When you're not all flailing about doing things to each other, be patient and take it in turns to watch while the other 'couple' get it on.

Role Play

This is where fantasies really become reality. It's the next step up from just imagining what it would be like actually playing out the roles with costumes, props and lots of acting. It's the part where you get the opportunity to let your partner share playing doctors and nurses, rather than just imagining what your cute GP would really be like, if he asked you to slip your clothes off and lie down. You don't have to be an Oscar-winning actor for this – you just need your imagination, a sense of humour and a naughty streak. This is very sexy, very private Am Dram. Lots of role play involves very traditional, slightly dated gender roles – Doctors and Nurses for example – or involve one partner being domi-nant or submissive in a way that wouldn't be acceptable or desirable in everyday life. But then that's the point really . . . And just like any theatrical production, a little planning helps things move along more smoothly.

- **Set your scene**
  Think about what you want to do and where best to do it. Want to play French maid? Set the scene in the dining room. Fancy your man as a really handy, handyman? Have him go outside and knock on the door for his appoint-ment, before you start the action. Whatever you choose it's always better to start the role play when you enter a room or sit down, rather than just try and suddenly begin – which will probably have you both in fits of giggles at how unnatural it feels! Or take your role play away from the home – in the garden, on the beach or in a hotel room.

- **Props**
  It's much more fun and easier to get into the role, if you equip yourselves with some props and costumes. It also gives your partner a visual feast and allows them to actu-ally believe that you are someone else during your role play. Buy, hire or put together an appropriate outfit. Wigs are also great; especially if you're role playing a schoolgirl or judge. And props – whether it's a toy stethoscope, a

cat-o'-nine tails whip, or a handyman's tool box, all add to the atmosphere and 'reality'.

- **Attitude**
Whatever characters you choose to adopt, you need to think the role and get yourself in the mood. Is your character innocent and sweet, dominating and stern or prim and posh? Try talking in the kind of voice that suits your character and use your body language to really feel the part. Give your character a new and appropriate name so that you can use it in your acting. One important thing: role play, especially when one or other of you is fully in the zone, can get a little steamy and during certain scenarios become more painful than you'd like or cause you distress. You must agree a 'stop' word between you. A word which can't get confused with anything you're doing like 'yes', 'harder' or 'carpet'! Agree a word like 'Marmite' or 'Radio' – anything that can be heard loud and clear if it all gets a bit too much for you. And don't be afraid to use it. Role play can and hopefully will transport you into another world – but it needs to be one of pleasure not distress.

And just like setting the scene, props and the right attitude are essential to the best role-play sessions, there are various little tricks and devices that can be used, as you please, to spice up a variety of scenarios.

- **Talking dirty**
Hopefully you're already communicating about sex, telling each other what you like – and don't like – and how

and what he could do to make it feel even better. Learn to up the stakes during role play. Gently at first. Ask him to put his finger inside you or to spank your bottom. And then introduce a few naughty words and phrases of your choice to notch things up a bit. Become a slut, a whore or a virgin. Think porn movie and tell him what a huge, hard juicy cock he has and what you want to do with it. Keep your voice sexy and low and encourage more dirty talk by asking your partner how it feels, how wet or horny they're feeling and if they want more or want it harder or faster.

- **Food play**
Food and sex have always been inextricably linked. Both arouse all our five senses of sight, touch, taste, smell and hearing and all are physically linked in the limbic system of the brain, which controls our emotional attitude and activity. Adventurous eaters and those who savour flavour often make exciting, sensual lovers, while fussy, fast eaters on a limited diet tend to be less hungry in the bedroom too . . .

Research has clearly shown people who enjoy their food and are willing to experiment are much more likely to savour a good lovemaking session, whereas those who are parsimonious about food or unwilling to try anything new, will tend to follow suit sexually. And then there is the terminology of eating and food, which is heavily linked with sex. Nibbling, biting, sucking, swallowing, licking and tasting are all words that lend themselves easily to both pleasures. For example, strawberries dipped in chocolate

– the strawberries, as with any red food, are supposed to remind us of the swollen lips of an engorged vagina and chocolate releases feel good endorphins into our bodies as well as being the only food that melts at room temperature. Introducing food into role play can definitely enhance your pleasure and arousal.

- **Sensory deprivation**
  Sensory deprivation is where you limit or impair one or more of your five senses – touch, hearing, smell, taste or vision – in order to enhance one or more of the other senses as a result. Sensory deprivation is incredibly arousing to some people, so bondage gear such as blindfolds and masks that cover the eyes and mouth work really well during sex play.

- **Leather and PVC**
  What is it about leather and PVC that makes us think of sex? Almost all fetish and bondage clothes are made of leather, rubber or PVC and even those who choose to forego BDSM find wearing something tight, sculpted and black makes us feel sexier. Much of it has to do with base animal instincts – the sense of wild, unabated sexiness by wearing or seeing someone wearing such a tight, soft and flexible material that belongs in a non-human world where sexual mores and niceties don't really exist. It's also plump with promise – it's usually contained by zips or lacing that beg to be undone and it clings to the body like a second skin leaving nothing to the imagination. Whether your role play includes full fetish gear or just an occasional leather

or faux leather prop, it definitely adds more than a spark of wickedness to the proceedings.

Suggested scenarios

I've listed a number of popular role-play scenarios and added a few new ones. These are just to fire up your imagination and give you a few ideas – just go for whatever turns you and your partner on. They're also not 'scripts' or meant to assume male/female role play – just suggestions. Your choice of dialogue and who plays which role is entirely up to you and your partner . . .

Mistress of discipline

Kit yourself in whatever leather or PVC kit you choose. Keep it black and disciplinarian – even a satin pencil or leather skirt and black shirt would be good. Make it tight rather than obviously revealing. And you definitely need black stockings and knee-high black boots. Arm yourself with a 'weapon' or two. A paddle, belt, hairbrush, whip and wrist restraints. Your partner should be dressed in a normal, casual way. Ask him to undress. Slowly. If he's not doing it to your satisfaction, insist that he tries again or he'll be punished. Crack your whip a few times to ensure he knows exactly who is in control and keep your voice low and firm. You are in charge and you can order him to do whatever you want. Once he is naked, ask him to watch you undress. Or command him to lie face down, while you blindfold him and bind his hands together behind his back. He is not allowed to squirm, writhe or make any sound. If he should even think about trying to move things along at his own pace, ensure that he knows that his subordination will be dealt with in a manner of your choice. You can then crack that whip, riding crop or paddle. This is meant to cause a little pain but it isn't meant to create weals on his back or his bottom and it's definitely not the time to let rip on any underlying grudges on him that may be lingering from the time you thought he was coming onto your best mate!

He'll beg you to stop, but unless he's actually using your chosen 'stop' word (see page 200) you must carry on. You'll only show him mercy when *you're* so aroused that he's going to have to be untied in order to have that immediate sex that you need right now!

Teacher and pupil

A gentler version of mistress of discipline, this seems to work best when you are the student and your partner is the teacher – for some reason your man dressed as a schoolboy will either look like one of The Crankies or have you in peals of laughter, before you've even got going! So get yourself kitted up in a gymslip or school skirt, white blouse, tie and knee socks. The idea here is to look a bit St Trinian's – dishevelled, smutty and more than a promise of naughtiness. You are, of course, in some trouble at school and your teacher must punish you appropriately. Or perhaps you have done especially well at a subject and your teacher wants you to see just how much he appreciates your efforts. Or indeed if you're having trouble with your homework or revision, he can share the benefit of his experience and wisdom with that too.

Seducing a virgin

Make sure you dress in prim and proper clothes, a blouse with maybe just a button undone at the neck. Either wear a Doris Day, fifties-style oh-so-innocent skirt or maybe a pencil skirt. You could have bare legs, sheer or opaque stockings or even knee socks. Sit with your partner on the sofa and tell him that you have something to confess. You've reached a certain age and while you're a woman of the world in many ways, there's one thing that hasn't happened to you yet. You're still a virgin and have been searching for the right man to deflower you. Try and keep it polite and coy – let your nerves show. Or be bolder and while keeping that sweet and innocent virginal accent, tell him something really dirty that you'd like him to do to you. Let your partner explain how gentle – or indeed how rough – he's going to be with you and let him explain what exactly you have been missing all those years and how he's going to rectify that unfortunate situation for you. He'll be writhing with desire – but make sure that you both keep the role play going for as long as you can to hold all that anticipation in place.

Lady of the manor

You are a very rich, very posh older woman living in a fabulous country pile – alone of course, apart from the occasional maid or butler. Dress accordingly – pile your hair up into a bun and accessorise a suit with a few brooches and a silk scarf (it can be used later as a blindfold!). Your partner might be the gardener – younger and a bit rough around the edges but always pleased to help out for little money and the privilege of serving you. But you're lonely and your sexy young gardener is working outside, tending your shrubbery in nothing more than a vest and a pair of jeans. You watch him as his strong hands tenderly prune your bush and his upper arm muscles ripple and glisten with sweat. You wonder what those hands would feel like running over your breasts, so you open the back door, call to him and invite him in for a refreshing cup of tea . . .

Sex worker

Arrange to meet your partner on a dark, secluded street corner not too far from your home (in a safe place, for obvious reasons). Get yourself kitted out in some, tight, revealing and slutty clothes. Wear stockings and suspenders, a too-short tight mini and a clashing silky top. Put on a big coat and stand around on the corner for a minute or two, getting yourself into the feel of the role. Your partner should arrive in his car, park a few feet away and watch you for a few minutes. Then he should pull up slowly in front of you, lower his car window and ask whether you're available for business and how much you cost. Quote him a price of your choice. He wants to know what he gets for his money. You open your coat and show him what he's going to get for his money. He might accept or you might negotiate for a moment or two, suggesting that you'll throw in a few extras for his trouble. While you drive home, keep in business-like, impersonal character while he tells you what he'd like you to do to him you assure him of ultimate customer satisfaction.

The librarian

You can start role playing this in a quiet corner of a bookshop or library, or if you have bookshelves at home use these as props, especially as you reach up high to get a book from the top shelf, revealing black lacy stocking tops under your prim skirt. Or maybe you'll be bending over to reach a book right over in the corner of the bookcase. You are efficient, organised and ever so slightly snobby. Your partner is looking for a book that you rather disapprove of (this one perhaps!) and you look down at him, over your thick-rimmed glasses, with thinly disguised disdain. You are in the business of organising important reference books, not providing salacious reading material for this impertinent young man. You ask him why he would want such a book? He says he is happy to tell you exactly why and suggests that you might feel a little more relaxed and comfortable, by letting your hair down (literally and physically!) and removing your glasses, while you sit down next to him on the big squishy sofa in the corner.

Doctors and nurses

There are few of us who haven't fantasised about dishy doctors or cute nurses – they're the stuff of old-fashioned romance novels. They have both power and command and caring, nurturing qualities. It's a heady combo. And for many of us, playing doctors and nurses while at primary school was our first taste of what it was like to 'flirt' with the opposite sex.

Both of you should dress up as medical practitioners. Him as a doctor, in a white coat and a stethoscope. You in a fancy dress nurse's costume or just use a simple cotton dress and apron and dress it up with a nurse's hat, fob watch, black stockings and flat shoes. Or you might want to play the patient as your doctor asks you to go behind the curtain, lie down and remove your top so he can check your heartbeat. Or you are a junior nurse with a major crush on the new, handsome and oh-so shy doctor that's just started working with you. Or perhaps he's cross and stern, rarely smiling and never notices you but is married to his career. Or gentle and caring and gives you the occasional lingering glance that makes you blush. Whatever scenario you choose, you need to find some sort of an excuse to ensure that you find a way to get him alone, so that he is in no doubt how you feel about him.

French maid

One of the most 'traditional' of role plays, there's something quaintly old-fashioned about playing the role of a French maid, so make the most of it. Your partner should be dressed beautifully in a dinner jacket and bow-tie or in a smoking jacket and cravat. Perhaps his hair is slicked back twenties style. You are a sexy little French maid, dressed in a way-too-short black frock, a white lacy apron and a floppy mop cap. Oh and uber-sexy stockings and suspenders and teeteringly high black shoes of course. There is virtually no costume site or shop which doesn't sell these maid outfits or pull some together from your own props cupboard. Your aim is to please your master by serving him drinks and food from your silver tray. You are an innocent employee, however naughtily you may be dressed and you would be shocked to your core if your master was to behave inappropriately with you. Which of course he is just about to do . . .

This is a great role play to introduce food – the more slippery, juicy and soft the better.

Sex slave

OK, you're the slave and your partner is the master. He is going to make sure you have the wildest of times and you have to follow his instructions and commands very carefully. You are completely naked – except perhaps for the odd ankle or wrist restraint or blindfold, as he wishes. He'll ask you something simple at first – fetch him a drink or stroke his shoulders. Then he gets bolder with his demands and warns you that if you don't comply, you'll get punished. Keep a few props like a hairbrush handy, just in case you are really naughty and don't do as you're asked. He'll tell you that you have been a very bad girl and just when he thinks you might be enjoying his sex play – he'll stop whatever he's doing and move onto something else. Remember that he is completely in control and it's his call as to whether you should be having pleasure or not.

Strangers in the night

Arrange to meet in a crowded bar, near to home if you can, and get there ten minutes before the appointed time. Grab yourself a bar stool and order yourself a drink. As he approaches, pretend you haven't noticed him. Look cool, calm and collected. Or nervous, apprehensive and flustered – whatever you fancy. He asks you if you'd like a drink. You might or you might not. Whatever you do, you don't bother swapping names or niceties – but move swiftly onto a discussion of how sexy he finds you and what he'd like to do to you. And you're clearly enjoying his flattery and dirty, whispered words. As you start to feel more aroused, one of you suggests that you get out of the bar and get yourselves a cab back to somewhere a little more private.

Naughty neighbour

You have noticed this cute guy that lives close to you. And you're pretty certain that he's noticed you too. But you're always rushing out to work and you never get a chance to say anything but a quick good morning to him. Anyway, you think he might have a girlfriend or be married so it's just a nice fantasy to have. This is a good scenario to play early in the evening just as twilight begins. You'll have come from work and decided to have a long, scented bath to help you unwind. You're just settling down with a good book with a glass of wine and a great CD, when there's a knock on the door. Although you're freshly scrubbed and smelling sweet, you're wearing nothing but a silk robe. You decide to see who could be knocking on your door and when you open it, there is your neighbour wondering if he could borrow a cup of sugar, as he seems to have run out. It would be rude to leave him on the doorstep while you sort out his cup of sugar, so you invite him in for a drink. You indulge in a little neighbourly chit chat while you casually let your robe drop open, so that he can see just what a good (or bad!) neighbour you really could be . . .

The horny handyman

Another traditional role-play scenario where you can either adopt the submissive role of the helpless housewife who, overwhelmed with loneliness, desire and gratitude, simply falls into the arms of this man who simply came around to sort out your leaky valve. Or you might want to adopt the dominant stance of insisting that you take this young and innocent apprentice plumber and show him a thing or two about how pipes really function. Whatever version you choose, you should encourage your partner to don a loose boiler suit – great for adding to the atmosphere and dropping in one fell swoop – as well as knocking on your door, tool box in hand. Keep a low sexy voice and even the most simple of tools for the job can sound suggestive and very, very naughty.

The polo player

This is a very *Officer and a Gentleman* or James Bond scenario and indeed can be played out with your partner as a captain of a cruise liner or an airline pilot. The main thing here is that, unusually for role play, he really gets to go to town on the dressing up. Suit, epaulettes and cap – whatever it takes to recreate the debonair, powerful and sexy man in charge.

Back to our polo player . . . This role suits a man with rugby player's thighs and a certain presence. You will be dressed in a pretty, floaty dress having decided to go to watch a polo match. You are attracted to one player in particular, with his smart white jodhpurs, bulging biceps and tan, weathered riding boots. How handsome he looks on his horse. But, no, he has had a fall and while there is no harm done, he needs to sit down and take a few minutes out. And there he is, sitting on your sofa, sipping a reviving drink, sweat gently glistening on his brow and arms and just a little turf smut on his cheek. His legs are slightly open, there's a gentle bulge just to the left of his tight white riding pants and he's thanking you profusely for coming to his rescue . . .

Sex Games

Playing manufactured sex games, rather than simple role play, is a great way to spice up your sex life, especially if you feel a bit uncomfortable or awkward about developing your own role-play scenario. Much of the imagination and perseverance to sustain a role play is done for you and there are some really fun games out there to fire up the juices. Games such as Nookii, Game for Sex and Monogamy are 'classics' of their type and readily available at reputable Internet sex toy sites like onjoy.com and sextoys.com

For those who want to develop their own versions, here are a few suggestions:

- **Roll the dice**

  Buy two of those giant dice from a toy shop and then cover the six numbers with labels of different, sexy body parts. Then take turns to throw two dice, to see what happens. You then get a pair of dice with two different sexy body parts on them. Clitoris and nipples for example. It's then up to you and your partner to invent a little sex play that involves ultimate pleasure while using both parts simultaneously!

- **Blind man's buff**

  An intriguing version of the children's game of Blind Man's Bluff. Only this time you ask your lover to strip, or gently help him remove his clothes. Then you put a blindfold on him and tell him that you're going to wrap him up. Using a combination of special bondage tape (that you can buy over the net at most sex toy shops) and standard cling film, you wrap the tape around his wrists – and ankles if you like – so that he can't protest and then proceed to wrap the rest of his body (not his face of course!) in the cling film, paying special attention to making it extra taut over his chest, bottom, thighs and penis. It's actually very sexy to see flesh bound through its transparent casing. Then writhe over him, so he can tantalisingly feel your flesh through the cling film but never really gets the usual sensation of skin touching skin.

- **Sexy Scrabble**

  Suggest to your partner that you play a game of Scrabble. Only this is no ordinary game of Scrabble – all the words have to be sex related and the naughtier the better. Use descriptive words – lick, nibble, suck as well as body parts. Don't fret if you don't have all the right letters – the message is more important than precise spelling. The winner gets to choose exactly which words on the board he or she gets to 'do' to you.

- **Strip poker**
  One of the classic sex games, this involves taking an item of clothing off for every hand that you lose during a game of poker. You can play this with a bunch of friends – which is probably how most of you remember it from something a bit daring during your time at college – but it's just as good when played by just you and your lover. Especially if you add in a few customised forfeits of your own. For example, you can insist on the order of clothes removal (always handy as it's never a pretty sight seeing a man in nothing but a pair of threadbare socks!) or you can stroke and lick whichever part of the body becomes exposed, but you'll stop the moment you see a sign of arousal like erect nipples or a moan of pleasure.

- **Peeping Tom**
  Get undressed as slowly and as sexily as possible and let him watch through a window or an open door. He needs to keep very quiet and still, as you 'don't know' that he's there, looking at you. When you've removed most or all of your clothes, lie down on the bed or sofa and start to masturbate.

Sex Toys

Sex toys come in a bewildering array of shapes and sizes and their uses are not always immediately obvious. Some look like they might cleave you in half, or are as small as your lipstick, others look rather beautiful but hugely expensive while some simply look like you might end up in your local A & E Department! But according to a recent sex survey, from Durex, more than one in five adults have used a vibrator. And these vibrators don't simply vibrate – they twist and turn, swivel and are designed to be used in your mouth, bottom, breasts, urethras and perineums as well as your clitoris and vagina.

The truth is that sex toys (a far better term than the rather unfortunate sounding 'sex aids' as they used to be called!) have been around for centuries. The ancient Greeks used them and sex toys have been found that are over two thousand years old. And in China, the third century Han Dynasty created dildos made from ivory and wood, many of which were double ended to accommodate two women at once!

By the mid-nineteenth century dildos were widely used and manufactured. The rubber model was introduced around 1859 with electrical devices following by the end of the century. Rather than giving sexual pleasure they were used as medical aids. Medical massage didn't have any stigma and was widely administered as a muscle relaxant and stress reliever.

The first patented steam-powered vibrator was developed in 1903 and such was the popularity of vibrators among women that they became the fifth household appliance to be electrified, beaten only by the sewing machine, fan, kettle and toaster!

When vibrators were portrayed as medical aids all was right with the world, then pornographers began to depict their actual use. Censors frowned on these blatant acts of female sexuality and the vibrator was driven underground until work by sexologists, including Alfred Kinsey in the 1950s brought female sexuality back into public discussion. And then of course, we went through the swinging sixties when sexuality became truly liberated and sex toys became ever more sophisticated and into the nineties when *Sex and the City* introduced us to the divine pleasures of the perfectly constructed and perennially popular, mainstream and wholly acceptable-to-own-one Rabbit.

Today's toys are more than simple playthings; they can improve vaginal muscle control and allow women who have never had an orgasm to experience one for the first time. Women often fall into two categories – those who would save their vibrator from their house if it were burning down and those who can't imagine what all the fuss is about. I want to take you through simple sex toys – and even those which sound more complicated often have cheaper versions for you to try out – so that you can learn to experiment with what takes your fancy, learn how to use them and find those that suit your needs and desires best. And while many of them are amazing used on your own, men are perennially fascinated by them, how you use them and what you can do with them to him. So once you've mastered the art, bring them into your sex play with your partner too. Just remember that anything that penetrates needs to used with a good water-based lubricant – for ease of use and ultimate pleasure.

Bondage play

I've called this bondage play, because most of the stuff that I talk about in this section is pretty much what you'll want to do at home. I cover some of the more 'hard-core' group fetish activities and S & M (sadism and masochism) in the next chapter. But for now, I am going to look at what is commonly known as BDSM (Bondage, Domination, Submission and Masochism). It's naughty enough and involves one of you being submissive (a sub) while the other is dominant (a dom). It involves a certain degree of pain and includes whipping, spanking, tying up and scratching. But it's sexier and less threatening – owing more to leather, high heels and silk than it does to gimp suits, ball gags and dungeons. It's highly arousing because it increases sexual tension in the nicest way – being at the mercy of someone else (or doing the controlling) when they are teasing, licking or penetrating you is exciting, edgy and wholly *not* what we do in everyday life. Causing pain, expecting servitude and physically restraining your partner do not make up a healthy relationship on a day-to-day basis!

The pain/pleasure threshold, on which all bondage play is based, can be an overwhelming sensation that will boost your orgasms to new levels, due to the brain releasing feel good chemicals called endorphins to help reduce the pain caused by a spank or slap. You may also enjoy seeing a temporary mark left on your lover's bottom or thigh due to the punishment you have meted out. Whipping, slapping or spanking your partner's bottom, thighs or legs will also heighten the nerve endings in the targeted area, making your lover's skin much more responsive to stroking, licking, biting, nibbling and scratching after it has been struck with a whip or paddle.

Bondage itself is the act of tying up your partner (or them tying you up) so that they are helpless, writhing and in your sexual control and command. You have the opportunity to act as the dominant partner (doing the tying) or the submissive partner (at their mercy). While the physical act of bondage – tying up your partner with bondage tape, a silk scarf or handcuffs, for example – is a major turn-on, the verbal form of bondage is just as exciting. Commanding your lover, or being told what to do by them, is an intensely sexy feeling that will lead you to do and command things you might normally be too embarrassed to mention. You can use bondage to act out role-play scenarios (such as those mentioned on page 198) or to pull apart or spread open parts of your lover's body. You can tie your partner to a chair, a bed or just use it to restrict normal movement.

- **Being a great dom**
  - o Be demanding and commanding – this is not a time to be polite.
  - o You must threaten punishment and then carry it out.
  - o Tease them to please them – unpredictability makes bondage play even sexier.

- **Being a great sub**
  - o You must be subservient and obedient at all times, unless you want to be punished.
  - o You must be polite and express gratitude at all times – before, during and after punishment.
  - o Make sure your body language reflects your servility – kneel down, look adoringly at your partner or stay on all fours.

Last word on bondage – always remember your chosen 'stop' word; don't tie someone up for too long; and be aware that your partner might get anxious or have a panic attack – so remember that you might just have to stop suddenly, however fantastic you're feeling.

Handcuffs

Handcuffs or arm restraints are essential in bondage play. Most handcuffs are made of leather, but depending on your preference you can go for the heavy duty, police variety (just don't lose the key!) or the furry, fun variety. You can also use special bondage tape or simply a silk or cotton scarf – anything that will keep your partner from moving their arms or hands, but won't actually stop their circulation altogether!

Blindfolds

Blindfolds add to the fun, because they work on sensory deprivation. Not being able to see what is happening to you, adds to the intensity of the feelings. Wearing a blindfold means that each lick, nibble and stroke is full of sensory surprise. You can buy leather, silk or sequinned blindfolds or just use a traditional scarf – you don't need fancy equipment for this sensation.

Paddles and whips

Paddles and whips are designed to help you and your partner straddle that pain–pleasure divide with varying degrees. Using whips and spanking paddles is a harmless and provocative way of spicing up your sex life and opening up new sexual avenues for you and your partner to explore. Indulge yourselves in some punishment role play by using a whip or spanking paddle to dish out small amounts of pain in response to naughty activities. No paddle? Use a hairbrush handle or a wooden spoon instead.

Harnesses and Strap-ons

Harnesses are designed to hold a dildo or vibrator in place, usually for pleasuring another person. Some harnesses can hold both an external and an internal (or two internal) dildos or vibrators. It's actually a misconception that strap-ons are lesbian devices; in fact they are used far more often by heterosexual women performing anal sex on their partner. They can be hugely expensive and some women just find them too uncomfortable to wear (and heavy dildos just have a habit of falling out!) but if you fancy trying one the **Vivid Designer Harness** range is worth a look.

Vibrators

And so to the biggest market and most popular form of sex toy available. Why? Because they are by far the easiest way to have a clitoral orgasm. By stimulating the head of the clitoris in an intense, rhythmical way it gives you a much easier, faster and more effective way to orgasm. Your partner's magic fingers or tongue might work wonders on your clitoris, but the truth is the quickest and simplest way to an orgasm is via the vibrator route. It may not be the most pleasurable sensation, in terms of that all-over fabulous orgasmic feeling that having sex with your lover brings – but hell, it's a fine alternative.

So what, amongst the dizzying array of shapes, colours, price points and promises are my own top recommendations? The best are available at sextoys.com or onjoy.com

- *The Rabbit* – this has to be top of the list, simply because it's the one women return to time and time again as the most enduringly satisfying vibrator on the market. It can be bought in many sizes – from bullet shaped, handbag size to super size and at prices from £15 to £100+. There are rechargeable versions, rabbits with extra bead stimulation in the shaft, and names like Jessica, Jack and Mr Big, but what they all have in common – hence their name – is the little rabbit ear attachment which vibrates at a rhythm to suit you, directly on your clitoris. Designed to be used along with the vibrating shaft, some women love their rabbit ears so much, that they only use this part of the vibrator. Like any other sort of vibrator, it can be an expensive matter of trial and error to find the right one for you – as so much depends on your own pleasure and comfort zone in relationship to the size, mechanics and in the case of the rabbit, the positioning and length of the rabbit ears in relationship to your clitoris. I suggest the **Rabbit Deluxe** or the **Eclipse 1050** but my own personal can't-live-without favourite is the **Slimline Passion Wave Jack Rabbit.**

- *Butterfly Vibrators* – Butterflies are vibrators specifically intended for clitoral stimulation. They are shaped like butterflies, with the main body concentrating the vibrations on the clitoris and the wings spreading additional vibrations around the genital region. Some of these can be strapped on, using a harness around your thighs. It's also hands free, so incredibly useful if you find operating the controls of a vibrator gives you tired arms! They cost between £10 and £50. My recommendation would be to go for the **Honeydew Butterfly.**

- *G-Spot Vibrators* – there is much more on the all-important G-spot on pages 149–54, but you can also buy specially angled vibrators that are designed to maximise stimulation to your G-spot. They look much like any other vibrator, but tend to be longer than normal and have a curved end to make sure that you hit the spot. My recommendation would be to go for the **Slim Stimulator G-Spot** or one of the **Rock Chick** versions, both from sextoys.com

- *Bullet Vibrators* – these little cuties are not much bigger than a lipstick, often made of metal and are very discreet – perfect as a travelling companion. They are designed to sit between the lips of the vagina and provide intense stimulation of your clitoris. They also work on your breasts, nipples and around the rim of your anus, providing a great buzz for you and your partner. There are some great ones made by **Candy Girl** and **Rock Chick**.

Dildos

Dildos are named after the Italian term *diletta*, meaning delight, and have the general shape and appearance of a penis. This can range from highly realistic to vaguely penis-like. They also vary in colour, from rainbow to natural skin tones and are made of rubber, latex, vinyl, plastic or jelly. There are also some rather beautiful ones around made of (toughened) glass that wouldn't look out of place on your window ledge or mantelpiece! They also vary enormously in size – from the gently realistic to porn star proportions. Although some dildos have built in vibrators, the point is that they generally don't vibrate but are designed to either go in a strap-on harness or be used manually as hard, penetrative stimulus. They are also known as dongs. They are best used while using a vibrator on your clitoris – as used on their own they can be a bit disappointing! The **Crystal Cote Dong** is a good one to try, being pretty tough and realistic looking. Another alternative is the rather beautifully named **Sensual Shapeshifter**. But the most important thing is that you find one that fits you well – they're like a perfect, customised penis – and getting the right shape and size is really important. Rather than spend a fortune finding out just what does suit you, try a six- or eight-inch version – it usually does the trick.

Clitoral stimulators

Clitoral stimulators are designed to directly stimulate the clitoris and while they usually vibrate, there are also non-powered clitoral stimulators that work by rubbing against the clitoris when walking or moving around. Clitoral stimulators come in both strap-on and hand-held varieties. The two most popular clitoral stimulators are the rabbits and the butterflies. If you want to try a vibrator designed especially for clitoral stimulation, try the **Waterproof Clitoral Hummer** designed for women, by women!

Butt plugs

Butt plugs are toys designed to be inserted into the anus to give anal pleasure without actual penetration. They can be simple 'A' shaped devices, realistically moulded penises, or exotic shapes. They feature a flange (a flared device to prevent them disappearing inside you!) on one end so that they don't slide inside the body and are available in a variety of materials including plastics, rubber and jelly. They must be used with a really good lubricant and are great for experimenting with, especially if this is your first time to anal sex. They leave your hands to do other stuff while they open up your rectum. Your partner will love you using one on him too, as they reach to the male G-spot – the prostate gland (see page 152).

Toys for boys

OK, I am pretty aware that I have neglected to say much about toys for guys (although you can have a lot of fun with the ones mentioned above) so let's just run through the top three toys for the boys . . .

1 *Fleshlight* – this looks like an ordinary flashlight (geddit?) but is actually a masturbation sleeve using very flesh-like soft silicone to imitate a vagina. All you have to do is put your penis in the hole at the end (and you customise the inside to be as tight, smooth or as ridged as you want it) and off you go. There are training versions of the flesh-light, varieties that look like mouths or rectums (as well as vaginas), transparent versions, so you can see yourself in action and a whole series of them designed and moulded by named, female porn stars. There is even a little receptacle at the end to collect your semen. As well as being the neatest little thing, it is also the world's number one best-selling male sex toy, so it looks like it might be your challenge to our much-loved Rabbit!

2 *Cock rings* – these are simple devices designed to keep blood engorged in the penis in order to hold an erection longer to better satisfy your partner. Some of them are scary looking things (to us women at least) made of leather

and metal like a cage, while others look more harmless – and probably more effective – and are made of silicone.

3 *Prostate stimulators* – these hand-held, angled toys are designed to go into your anus for direct stimulation onto your prostate gland, or G-spot. The best ones vibrate and can make your orgasms explosive!

Luxury toys

There are a whole host of luxury sex toys out there on the market. And by luxury, I don't just mean seriously expensive – some of the platinum versions cost up to £4000 – but rather beautiful, designer-inspired, amazing objects in their own right. The thing about luxury toys is that the more expensive they become, the less they look like what they are meant to do. Very few look like a penis – most are slightly alien-like, or look like a cigar case or a mobile phone. Some are designed, in fact, to work with your mobile phone or your MP3 player. And many are, sadly, a triumph of form over function. However, a number of them have been developed clinically, using the most advanced technology available and medical grade silicone in beautiful jewel-like colours, and amazingly they work just as they should – delivering first-class orgasms. At a first-class price of course.

   None of my special favourites will leave you much change from £100, but all these are guaranteed to deliver amazing service and somehow because they are intrinsically beautiful objects in themselves, there is something very special about using them that adds to your pleasure. For my money, buying just one of these will serve you well. They tend to be water-proof, discreet and rechargeable. And added to your favourite, penis-shaped vibrator, you will have an orgasmic repertoire on your hands for every mood.

- **Sasi by Je Joue** – this is shaped like a large, very pretty, double pebble with a ball bearing underneath its oh-so-soft silicone skin. It both vibrates against your vulva and the little ball bearing is the closest that any toy, in my view, has come to simulating oral sex. There are two modes – favourite, which goes through all the functions – and customised mode, which you can adapt to your own needs, and it remembers what you like as well as having a handy 'don't stop' button.

- **We-vibe** – this cute little purple affair manages to work in harmony between the G-spot and your clitoris. It has two speeds and not only does it manage (successfully) to deliver two sorts of stimulation at the same time, it can also be used when you are having sex with your partner, so that you can have it stimulating your clitoris while the G-spot part stimulates the shaft of your lover's penis during sex. You can also walk around the house while wearing it, without anyone knowing it and you can give your pelvic floor muscles a workout at the same time. Ingenious!

- **Lelo Iris** – this is sexy and pleasing to look at – yet still powerful and boasts a pair of individually balanced vibra-tor motors working in harmony, making for deep and powerful vibrations. It has a special locking dial feature to save you activating it by accident. So no more excuses about your 'electric toothbrush' going off when you're travelling! You get five different patterns – from gentle stimulation to a much more powerful vibe.

- **Jimmy Jane Little Chroma** – this is the little vibrator allegedly beloved by Kate Moss and it's certainly discreet in size. Not quite as quiet as the manufacturers would have us believe, it is waterproof and offers a deep, resonant vibration. It's very lightweight – made of anodised aluminium – rather than jelly and can be heated up or cooled down. It's pretty effective, in a low-key way, and certainly looks absolutely gorgeous as well.

- **OhMiBod** – this is a lot of fun, looks sleek and lovely and works. So it ticks most of the boxes – although perhaps not quite as effective at achieving the perfect orgasm as the vibes listed above. The OhMiBod combines elegant design with your favourite music downloaded to your MP3 player and is especially compatible with an iPod. And if you've got some special music on your MP3, which you might listen to while using your usual vibrator, the OhMiBod seamlessly allows you to do both at the same time.

While I hope I've covered most of what you might want in your regular sex lives here, I am aware that some of you will want to get on to some more X-rated stuff and really push a few boundaries, so read on . . .

8 X-Rated: the Kinky Stuff

This is always going to be a tough area to get right. Many of the previous chapters in this book will have contained certain suggestions and advice that will have shocked some of you or made you think 'no way' before you even got to this chapter. For others, anything I am going to suggest here will appear tame, mundane or part of your regular sex lives and add little to your repertoire. You might think that I haven't gone 'far enough'. That's the problem with writing about sex – not only is one man (or woman's) meat another man's poison, what is acceptable, fabulous and regular to one couple can appear deeply unappetising to another couple.

So, forgive me for calling this the 'X-rated' section. And for describing certain practices as 'kinky'. All I have attempted here is to go into some further detail on what is not generally commonplace for an average couple – whoever or whatever – they might be. To offer up explanations for things that you may or may not have heard of or not understand. And to describe the pros and cons of taking your sex life a step or two further. As I said in the introduction to this book, anything that goes on between two consenting adults in the privacy of their own homes (and lots of variations on that scenario – as in outside their homes and involving other consenting adults) that doesn't cause enduring physical or emotional harm to you or others involved with your sexual lives, which may still be considered taboo in some circles, should most definitely be up for discussion and consideration.

There are also certain sexual practices, of course, that in my view, are simply best avoided. It goes without saying that anything involving children or animals is completely out of the question. And nor indeed are certain sexual practices like autoerotic asphyxiation (the act of choking someone until they are near death to intensify their orgasm) or edge play, which is sex involving possible serious injury or even death. Great sex is about sublime pleasure, enormous fun and absolute fulfilment. It should never, ever be about violation, emotional or physical abuse or cruelty to animals or children or a life-threatening activity.

There's a whole world of dodgy sex acts out there and many, many slang expressions for them. Of course, the Internet displays a huge range of sexual practices and predilections. Some of it is mildly titillating, some seriously gross and much of it illegal. It's out there if you want to take a look. I'll just conclude this book with a few of the more 'acceptable' sexual practices that you might want to experiment with or that you are just curious to know a little more about.

Anal sex

Anal sex is becoming so 'mainstream' now that maybe it doesn't really belong in the X-rated chapter at all. Research has shown that around 35% of heterosexual couples have tried anal sex and around half of them continue to do it pretty regularly. But it's still something that many women don't want to try for the obvious reasons – your anus is smaller, tighter, drier than your vagina and we're meant to poo out of it, not have sex with it. And yet, few of us will not have met a guy who really wants to try anal sex. Indeed, may have pestered us to try it. And there are men out there who are not beyond trying the 'whoops, wrong hole' trick during sex. And if this has happened to you, you'll know that a sharp, penetrative and clumsy thrust into your unlubricated bottom is way more pain than pleasure!

Truth is, that if done properly, many women enjoy anal sex. Your rectum being penetrated can be a really pleasurable, 'full' feeling, especially if your man can use his finger inside your vagina and/or on your clitoris too. The secret to enjoyable anal sex lies in patience and preparation. You need to use a silicone-based lube – and plenty of it. The sphincter muscles in the anus are like one of the old-fashioned tea-towel holders in reverse and are meant for pushing things *out*, not pulling them in, so it's essential to feel as relaxed as possible and get your partner to use his fingers to gently soften the muscles first. It often feels uncomfortable to start with – whether it's your lover's fingers or his penis – as it feels as if there is an obstructive ridge to pass through before it becomes more comfortable. That's why relaxing – both emotionally and physically – is so important as it helps this process along. And whether you're squeamish or not, anal sex is always more pleasant if you have a freshly showered bottom. Even so, anal sex is a breeding ground for sexually transmitted infections, so using a condom is always a good idea.

The most comfortable positions for anal sex are doggy style or missionary – with your knees pulled back and your feet on your lover's shoulders. Get your partner to put lubrication on his penis and your anus and to proceed with short, slow and gentle thrusts. If you feel more pain than pleasure, agree beforehand that you'll stop as soon as you say so. It's really important that your sphincter muscles are relaxed (as well as your attitude) as if they seize up, it can become painful again. Communicate with your partner at all times and don't let either of you have high expectations, especially if this is your first time, as it can often take a few attempts to allow your partner to fully penetrate.

Some women find that having an orgasm before anal sex helps relax their sphincter muscles. Others use desensitising anal cream. Frankly, although this numbs the pain it also numbs the pleasure and if it's really hurting too much, it's a sign to stop before you do any internal damage – and disguising that with a desensitising cream is not a good idea.

An alternative to anal sex is to use a butt plug. These have flared ends (so they can't disappear inside you) and leave your lover's hands to get on with other stuff. Get your lover to apply some silicone-based lubrication to both the plug and the rim of your anus. If he gently pushes the plug, your bottom should suck in the plug a little – they don't go too far in. You simply leave it there and enjoy having sex any other which way. If it isn't inserted at just the right depth, it can feel uncomfortable, so it might not be for you.

Another newer alternative is to use anal beads. These special beads are designed to take advantage of the pleasant sensations that can occur as your sphincter muscles open and close around a series of small round objects. These beads, which might be even sized, or graduated in size, are spaced along a stalk or a cord. They are gentler than a butt plug and create a different kind of sensation as when each bead is inserted the sphincter muscles contract and then relax around each individual bead. Pulling them out during an orgasm can really heighten the sensation too.

If anal sex isn't for you – or even if it is – you might enjoy rimming. Rimming is oral anal stimulation and involves thrusting your stiff tongue into the anal passage, as if it were a penis. Or you could just try licking around the area with your tongue and flicking it in and out of the opening. The anus is rich with nerve endings and this in itself can bring a lot of unexpected pleasure for both partners.

S & M

S & M, or Sadism and Masochism – or just sadomasochism – is a more gritty, more painful and more full on activity than bondage and domination. It's like advanced bondage and often involves seriously strange and scary paraphernalia like gimp masks and vicious-looking nipple clamps. If bondage and spanking games are soft porn, then S & M 'proper' is like hardcore porn and less than 10% of couples who enjoy bondage games go onto the more serious side of sadomasochism.

Basically, sadism involves inflicting pain on others to feel aroused while masochism is the pleasure you get from pain being inflicted on you by your partner. But there's also a darker side of S & M involving extreme power and domination – which it has in common with bondage games, but it tends to be more intense in both equipment, practice and fervour. It can also be quite toxic and addictive, so if you find your sex life veering further into using pain for pleasure and you don't feel comfortable about it, it's time to communicate your feelings with your partner. Like any other form of 'kinky' sex practice, its pleasure is almost entirely dictated by trust, communication and honesty.

At its best S & M can be quite glamorous and pantomime-like and if you fancy a journey into its possibilities, then either invest in a few of the more bizarre-looking bits of kit offered on many websites or go along to an established and reputable fetish club, like The Torture Garden. Everyone dresses up and it can be a fabulous visual feast if nothing else.

Fisting

Fisting involves inserting a hand into the vagina or rectum. Contrary to its name, fisting does not actually involve forcing a clenched fist into the vagina or rectum. Instead, all five fingers are kept straight and held as close together as possible. This forms a beak-like stricture, known as a 'silent duck'. Indeed when done correctly, your hand should look exactly like a hand cartoon duck, where if you opened your fingers and thumb together, you'd expect to be making a quack-quack sound!

You then slowly insert your hand into a very well-lubricated vagina. Your hand will naturally curl up once inside. Once you are inside you can hold still, gently move in and out, or gently rotate your wrist.

Fisting is best done very slowly and only when highly aroused and very well-lubricated. Many women find the feeling just too intense, so be patient, take your time and be ultra aware of when it's time to stop.

'Lesbian' sex

Girl-on-girl action has long been a common male fantasy (see page 189) but it's also something that many women want to try. It can feel very natural as we are understandably far more familiar with a woman's body and her needs and desires than those of a man. You might well have had an experimental romp in bed with another girl before you had any sexual experience with a man. But if you're in a faithful heterosexual relationship, does it even count as infidelity? The jury's out on this – it's your call – but if you feel that there's someone you trust and fancy and she might feel the same way, then why not give it a go? It can be immensely pleasurable as it can be a more tender and less urgent experience than sex with a man. But a word of warning – just because you and a girlfriend get on like a house on fire, tell each other everything and put the world to rights over a bottle of wine on a regular basis, she may still be completely shocked by the idea that you want sex with her, so tread very carefully on this one.

And don't let your partner think that this is a spectator sport. Many men love the idea of you getting it on with another woman so as (a) they can watch or (b) with luck they'll be invited to join in. Being bi-curious or having sexual urges for another woman is totally understandable, if a little daunting, and is probably best performed in private for the first time.

Watersports

Watersports, also known as golden showers, is the act of peeing on your partner, or having them pee on you. It's correct term is *urolagnia* from the Greek, urine and *lagneia* meaning lust. The most common form such play takes is for one partner to pee in such a way that the other partner can see and or feel the golden shower of urine.

Curiously many people find watersports to be one of the most taboo areas of sex play, which given that peeing is a wholly natural and necessary act and that urine itself is virtually sterile, it's surprising it's not more commonplace in our repertoires.

It's best done when your bladder is full, obviously, and can be done while standing or sitting over the toilet, while your partner sits down with their legs open, with the aim, literally, of peeing directly on to his penis or her vagina. It can also be done in the bath – or pretty much anywhere where you can clean up easily enough.

I could go on and on here, delving ever deeper into some of the more unusual sexual practices, but given that this is a book which takes you from the simple pleasures of a kiss, through the myriad treats in store for you during foreplay, the whys and wherefores of an orgasm and much more, I don't want to dwell on areas of sexuality which some might find offensive, threatening or simply unappetising.

I set out to write a book that was informative, straight-forward and with enough detail to give you plenty of food for thought. No book can be definitive, but I trust you have found what you have read enlightening, enjoyable and entertaining.

Whatever sexual skills and challenges you have learnt from this book, always remind yourself that good sex is all about having fun and great sex, while it might need a little more practice (hurrah!), is the ultimate pleasure zone that we all deserve.

Useful Websites

Typing the word 'sex' into your search engine will yield literally millions of results. In fact it is in the top ten most commonly searched-for words – with other sexual terms like 'porn' and 'pussy' making up most of the others! So, where to go if you just want some basic information?

The BBC website offers up some plain talking, reliable information while Wikipedia is great for clinical definitions of some of the terminology that you might not be familiar with. iVillage also has regular and entertaining articles on sex and relationships.

www.bbc.co.uk
www.wikipedia.com
www.ivillage.co.uk

Some of the larger sex toy websites also offer up copious and reputable information, ranging from videos on how to use some of the sex toys that they sell to articles on sexual health.

www.sextoys.co.uk
www.lovehoney.co.uk
www.onjoy.co.uk

There's also a huge number of websites simply selling sex toys and games of every variety. Some are a bit daunting and overwhelming, but I do recommend:

www.jejoue.com
www.ohmibod.com
www.lelo.com
www.funfactory.co.uk
www.jimmyjane.com
www.nookii.com

Index

Index

Index

roundabout kiss 58
routine 43, 81

S & M (sadomasochism) 185, 189,
   217, 233–4
safe sex 4–9, 43, 49
Sasi by Je Joue 227
scents 18, 19
Scrabble 213–14
sea 132–3
security 52
seduction 52, 65
see-saw position 126–7
self-consciousness 103, 197
self-esteem 45
semen 79, 86, 141, 152, 162
sense of humour 13, 16, 36
sensitivity 48
   female genitals 74, 81, 83, 84, 92,
     141
   G-spot 151, 152
   over-sensitivity 27–8, 79, 90, 92
   penis head 77–8
   prostate gland 153
   sensitive spots 66, 67, 68
sensory deprivation 202, 219
serotonin 55, 156
sex appeal 14–15, 31
sex drive 29–32, 49, 180
   mismatched 29–30
sex slave role play 209
sex toys 31, 143, 176, 215–28
   buying 212, 239–40
   hygiene 8
   luxury 226–8
sex worker role play 206–7
sexual appetite 32
sexual attraction 12–20
sexual chemistry 11–20, 30, 34, 37,
   55, 197
sexual health 4–9
sexual performance 20–29
sexual response cycle 140–41, 158
sexual tension 45, 48, 217
sexually transmitted infections 4–7,
   35, 232
showers 43, 48, 92
   golden, *see* watersports
side-by-side position 29, 108–9

sitting on top 24, 29, 33
size 21–9
   incompatibility 22
Skene's glands 162
skin 66, 140
skin-to-skin contact 103
smell 18, 19–20, 55
smile 15, 16
smoking 60
snake kiss 59–60
snogging 56, 57–8, 111
   practising 61
soul kiss 57
spanking 185, 189, 194–5, 217, 218
   paddles 220
splitting the bamboo 121
spontaneity 4, 67, 75, 111
spooning 108–9, 173–4
squeeze technique 163, 165
starfish position 123–4
'stop now' word 8, 21, 200, 204, 219
strangers, sex with:
   fantasy 184, 187–8
   role play 209–10
strap-ons 220, 223, 224
stress 21, 30, 39, 48, 70, 139, 144,
   147, 163, 167
strip poker 214
sub-conscious 13, 17–20
submission 91, 107, 195
   bondage play 217–19
   role play 199
sucking 36, 94
sun loungers 119, 132
swinging 197

tactile person 15
talking 2, 31, 33, 103, 167
   see also communication
talking dirty 54, 64–6, 166, 167,
   174, 200–201, 210
Taoism 147, 148, 165
teacher and pupil role play 204–5
teasing 34, 52, 82, 88, 93, 105, 185,
   218
teasing kiss 59
testicles 47, 48, 107, 140
   massaging 71–2
   oral sex 88, 91

247